Around the turn of the century, the photographer-at-work often became a subject in itself. The photographer in the picture is thought to be Edward Rollins, one of five professional photographers in Woodstock. From the Wetherell Collection, courtesy of Woodstock Historical Society

The Willimantic Chronicle *is proud to sponsor this special limited edition of*

Mills and Meadows: A Pictorial History of Northeast Connecticut.

We dedicate this book to the residents of

Tolland and Windham Counties — past, present, and future.

Proceeds from the sale of this volume will benefit the Windham Textile and History Museum.

the Chronicle

YOUR HOMETOWN PAPER SINCE 1877 ★ PUBLISHED DAILY IN WILLIMANTIC, CONN.

One of these photographers—probably the man on the left—has just set up his camera and rejoined the other members of this Putnam photography club to pose for a picture. In the 1880s, cameras were sufficiently portable to allow photographers to go on outings and capture the places and people of Northeast Connecticut—including themselves.
Courtesy of Aspinock Historical Society of Putnam

MILLS AND MEADOWS

A PICTORIAL HISTORY OF NORTHEAST CONNECTICUT

BRUCE M. STAVE and MICHELE PALMER

THE
DONNING COMPANY
PUBLISHERS

The Donning Company/Publishers
184 Business Park Drive, Suite 106
Virginia Beach, Virginia 23462

Richard A. Horwege, Editor
Mary–Eliza Midgett, Designer
Debra Y. Quesnel, Project Director

Library of Congress Cataloging in Publication Data:

Stave, Bruce M.
    Mills and meadows : a pictorial history of northeast Connecticut/
by Bruce M. Stave and Michele Palmer.
        p. cm.
    Includes bibliographical references and index.
    ISBN 0-89865-813-6 (Limited ed.)
      1. Tolland County (Conn.)—History, Local—Pictorial works.
2. Windham County (Conn.)—History, Local—Pictorial works.
I. Palmer, Michele. II. Title.
F102.T6S73 1991
974.6'43'00222—dc20   90-27387
                                                              CIP

Printed in the United States of America

CONTENTS

Foreword by Lucy Bartlett Crosbie   11

Preface   13

Acknowledgments   14

Chapter 1   CONNECTICUT'S COUNTRYSIDE   17

Chapter 2   MILLS: THE MAN-MADE LANDSCAPE   35

Chapter 3   GATHERING PLACES: MAIN STREETS AND TOWN GREENS   57

Chapter 4   ON THE ROAD   73

Chapter 5   SCHOOLS AND SOCIETY   95

Chapter 6   UPROOTED AND TRANSPLANTED   117

Chapter 7   PLAYING AROUND   133

Chapter 8   THE SKY IS FALLING   147

Chapter 9   WAR AND COMMUNITY   159

Chapter 10 PEOPLE AND POLITICS   169

Bibliography   187

Index   188

About the Authors   192

TOLLAND COUNTY

WINDHAM COUNTY

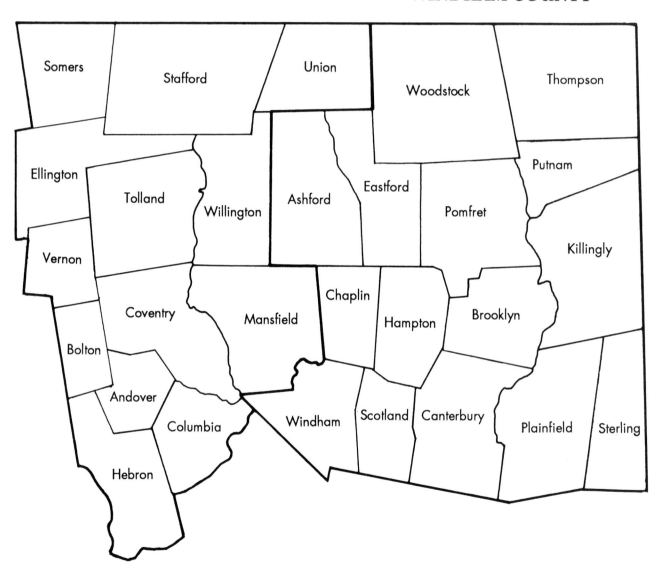

NORTHEAST CONNECTICUT TOWNS
THEIR ESTABLISHMENT, AND ORIGINS OF NAMES

TOWNS	YEAR ESTABLISHED	PARENT TOWN	ORIGINS OF NAMES
Andover	1848	Coventry Hebron	perhaps from Andover, Mass.
Ashford	1714	- - - - -	probably from Ashford in Kent, England
Bolton	1720	- - - - -	from Bolton in Lancashire, England or the Duke of Bolton
Brooklyn	1786	Pomfret Canterbury	from brook line (the Quinebaug)
Canterbury	1703	Plainfield	from Canterbury in Kent, England
Chaplin	1822	Windham Hampton Mansfield	from its deacon, Benjamin Chaplin
Columbia	1804	Lebanon	given the poetic name for the United States
Coventry	1712	- - - - -	from Coventry in Warwickshire, England
Eastford	1847	Ashford	named as east parish of Ashford
Ellington	1786	East Windsor	from Ellington in Yorks or Hunts, England
Hampton	1786	Windham Pomfret Brooklyn Canterbury Mansfield	from Hampton in Middlesex, England
Hebron	1708	- - - - -	from Hebrew, Hebron; meaning "An association," "a league," and "confederacy."
Killingly	1708	- - - - -	from Killingly manor near Pontefract, Yorkshire, England
Mansfield	1702	Windham	from Major Moses Mansfield
Plainfield	1699	- - - - -	name descriptive
Pomfret	1713	- - - - -	from Pontefract in Yorkshire, England
Putnam	1855	Thompson Pomfret Killingly	from Israel Putnam
Scotland	1857	Windham	named by first settler, Magoon, a Scot
Somers	1734	Enfield	part of Massachusetts until 1749, from Lord Somers
Stafford	1719	- - - - -	from Stafford, town in Staffordshire, England
Sterling	1794	Voluntown	from Dr. John Sterling, a resident
Thompson	1785	Killingly	from its chief owner, Sir Robert Thompson
Tolland	1715	- - - - -	from Tolland in Somersetshire, England
Union	1734	- - - - -	as "Union Lands"
Vernon	1808	Bolton	probably from the home of Washington at Mount Vernon
Willington	1727	- - - - -	from Wellington in Somersetshire, England
Windham	1692	- - - - -	from Windham in Sussex, England, or from Wymondham in Norfolk, England
Woodstock	1690	- - - - -	part of Massachusetts until 1749, from Woodstock in Oxfordshire, England

Sources: "Connecticut Towns, and Their Establishment," compiled by Ann P. Barry, Senior Reference Librarian, Archives, History and Genealogy Unit, Connecticut State Library, GS74-1985; *Connecticut State Register and Manual*, 1985, pp. 605-611.

POPULATION BY TOWN, 1790-1990
Northeast Connecticut
Tolland and Windham Counties

	1790	1800	1810	1820	1830	1840	1850	1860	1870	1880
Andover							500	518	461	428
Ashford	2,583	2,445	2,532	2,778	2,661	2,651	1,295	1,231	1,241	1,041
Bolton	1,293	1,452	700	731	744	739	600	680	576	512
Brooklyn	1,328	1,202	1,200	1,264	1,451	1,488	1,514	2,132	2,354	2,308
Canterbury	1,881	1,812	1,812	1,984	1,880	1,791	1,669	1,592	1,543	1,272
Chaplin					807	794	796	788	704	627
Columbia			834	941	962	842	876	854	891	757
Coventry	2,130	2,021	1,938	2,058	2,119	2,018	1,984	2,091	2,057	2,043
Eastford							1,127	1,006	984	855
Ellington	1,056	1,209	1,344	1,196	1,455	1,356	1,399	1,510	1,452	1,569
Hampton	1,332	1,379	1,274	1,313	1,101	1,166	946	989	891	827
Hebron	2,234	2,266	2,002	2,094	1,937	1,726	1,345	1,425	1,279	1,243
Killingly	2,166	2,279	2,512	2,803	3,257	3,685	4,543	4,960	5,712	6,921
Mansfield	2,635	2,560	2,570	2,993	2,661	2,276	2,517	2,194	2,401	2,154
Plainfield	1,713	1,619	1,738	2,097	2,289	2,383	2,732	3,665	4,521	4,021
Pomfret	1,768	1,802	1,905	2,042	1,978	1,868	1,848	1,660	1,488	1,470
Putnam								2,208	4,192	5,827
Scotland								735	643	590
Somers	1,127	1,353	1,210	1,306	1,429	1,621	1,508	1,511	1,247	1,242
Stafford	1,885	2,345	2,235	2,369	2,515	2,469	2,940	3,400	3,405	4,455
Sterling		908	1,101	1,200	1,240	1,099	1,025	1,050	1,022	957
Thompson	2,267	2,341	2,467	2,928	3,380	3,535	4,638	3,995	3,804	5,051
Tolland	1,538	1,638	1,610	1,607	1,698	1,566	1,406	1,310	1,269	1,169
Union	630	767	752	757	711	669	728	732	627	539
Vernon			827	966	1,164	1,430	2,900	3,833	5,446	6,915
Willington	1,212	1,278	1,161	1,246	1,305	1,268	1,388	1,166	942	1,086
Windham	2,765	2,644	2,416	2,489	2,812	3,382	4,503	4,261	5,412	8,264
Woodstock	2,445	2,463	2,654	3,017	2,917	3,053	3,381	3,285	2,955	2,639

Sources: *Connecticut State Register and Manual*, 1983,
The Hartford Courant, January 25, 1991.

1890	1900	1910	1920	1930	1940	1950	1960	1970	1980	1990
401	385	371	389	430	560	1,034	1,771	2,099	2,144	2,540
778	757	668	673	726	704	845	1,315	2,156	3,221	3,765
452	457	433	448	504	728	1,279	2,933	3,691	3,951	4,575
2,628	2,358	1,858	1,655	2,250	2,403	2,652	3,312	4,965	5,691	6,681
947	876	868	896	942	992	1,321	1,857	2,673	3,426	4,467
542	529	435	385	414	489	712	1,230	1,621	1,793	2,048
740	655	646	706	648	853	1,327	2,163	3,129	3,386	4,510
1,875	1,632	1,606	1,582	1,554	2,102	4,043	6,356	8,140	8,895	10,063
561	523	513	496	529	496	598	746	922	1,028	1,314
1,539	1,829	1,999	2,127	2,253	2,479	3,099	5,580	7,707	9,711	11,197
632	629	583	475	511	535	672	934	1,129	1,322	1,578
1,039	1,016	894	915	879	999	1,320	1,819	3,815	5,453	7,079
7,027	6,835	6,564	8,178	8,852	9,547	10,015	11,298	13,573	14,519	15,889
1,911	1,827	1,977	2,574	3,349	4,559	10,008	14,638	19,994	20,634	21,103
4,582	4,821	6,719	7,926	8,027	7,613	8,071	8,884	11,957	12,774	14,363
1,471	1,831	1,857	1,454	1,617	1,710	2,018	2,136	2,529	2,775	3,102
6,512	7,348	7,280	8,397	8,099	8,692	9,304	8,412	8,598	8,580	9,031
506	471	476	391	402	478	513	684	1,022	1,072	1,215
1,407	1,593	1,653	1,673	1,917	2,114	2,631	3,702	6,893	8,473	9,108
4,535	4,297	5,233	5,407	5,949	5,835	6,471	7,476	8,680	9,268	11,091
1,051	1,209	1,283	1,266	1,233	1,251	1,298	1,397	1,853	1,791	2,357
5,580	6,442	4,804	5,055	4,999	5,577	5,585	6,217	7,580	8,141	8,668
1,037	1,036	1,126	1,040	1,064	1,192	1,659	2,950	7,857	9,694	11,001
431	428	322	257	196	234	261	383	443	546	612
8,808	8,483	9,087	8,898	8,703	8,978	10,115	16,961	27,237	27,974	29,841
906	885	1,112	1,200	1,213	1,233	1,462	2,005	3,755	4,694	5,979
10,032	10,137	12,604	13,801	13,773	13,824	15,884	16,973	19,626	21,062	22,039
2,309	2,095	1,849	1,767	1,712	1,912	2,271	3,177	4,311	5,117	6,008

The Bolton Quarry, shown in this 1836 engraving by John Warner Barber produced a stone similar to slate, called quartzite, which was used as flagstone to pave the streets of Hartford and other large East Coast cities. Although this particular quarry is no longer mined, there are still active quarries in Bolton today.

FOREWORD

Mills and Meadows: A Pictorial History of Northeast Connecticut is being published on the eve of the 115th anniversary of the *Willimantic Chronicle,* which has underwritten the cost of this book, for the benefit of the Windham Textile and History Museum. The twenty-eight towns of Tolland and Windham counties are rich in history and their origins date back more than a century before the founding of the nation. This small corner at the northeastern edge of the country is as quintessentially American as any area of the country.

We hope these pictures will entice people, especially students, (the most visually oriented generation of youngsters since the invention of moveable type) to step into the past and judge for themselves what they can learn from it.

Photography was officially born in Paris in 1839 with what inventor Louis Jacques Daguerre called "a chemical and physical process which gives nature the ability to reproduce herself." After daguerreotypes, photography evolved to wet-collodian glass-plate negatives which could be reproduced endlessly, and then to dry plates and, eventually, modern roll film.

The daguerreotype was a medium so easily mastered that by 1850 more than thirty professional photographers were advertising in Boston newspapers. They and their successors in New England took thousands of pictures capturing the spirit and character of the people in the nineteenth century and the world in which they lived. Amateur photographers began recording the motionless world shown in these pages particularly after George Eastman introduced the Kodak hand camera in 1888 with the guarantee, "You press the button, we do the rest."

Most of the pictures in this book, drawn from public and private collections, have never before been published and, with few exceptions, we do not know the names of the photographers who took them. Few of these photographers probably ever paused to consider that what they were recording would vanish. None of us thinks, as we look around us, that what we see may be greatly altered in a decade, and often unrecognizable in fifty years. Most of the photog-raphers and the people who posed for them are now dead. The world they inhabited is gone: but their images survive.

Here, forever posed in one attitude, are factory workers at their machines, farmers in their fields. Children play in dusty streets, horse-drawn wagons make their rounds, and men march off to war. The pictures record the region's traditional life and the changes that were inexorably altering its character.

John McDonald, my great-grandfather, learned the printer's trade in his hometown of Danielson, and according to a Windham County history "saved his money and went west to Willimantic where he started the *Chronicle* in 1877."

My son and I are the fourth and fifth generations of his family to serve as publishers of the newspaper. We are pleased to join the distinguished authors of the text of *Mills and Meadows* in presenting the work of these early and contemporary photographers whose legacy is an enduring record of Northeast Connecticut.

Lucy Bartlett Crosbie

11

The Nathan Hale Homestead in Coventry was something of a touris[t]
attraction even in the early nineteenth century when artist/historia[n]
John Warner Barber drew this view. The fence encloses the compou[nd]
where Hale used to keep nightwatch over his family's sheep. When
the Revolutionary War broke out, Hale served as a captain under C[olonel]
Thomas Knowlton of Ashford. He was only twenty-one when he wa[s]
captured and executed by the British for spying. His famous last
words were reputed to be: "I only regret that I have but one life to
lose for my country." Whether accurate or not, the statement has
become part of the myth and lore of American history.

PREFACE

his book is a labor of love.
While neither author is a native of Northeast Connecticut, both are longtime residents of the region and harbor a special affinity for its character and charm. One is a historian and writer, the other a writer and artist. We have tried to combine our respective skills to produce a volume which captures the special qualities of Connecticut's northeast corner, while simultaneously placing them in a broad and meaningful historical framework.

Since this is a pictorial history, we attempt to present the reader with a visual appreciation of the area's history. Through chapter introductions and captions, our words try to offer a context for what you will see. To offer the widest possible scope and to provide in-depth coverage of our themes, the book is organized into topical chapters. By necessity, this involved a certain selectivity. The historian always must make such selections and we believe ours will provide not only a reasonable, but especially fruitful, approach to the history of Northeast Connecticut. The topics we have identified are: the region's rural character, the man-made landscape, particularly the role of the textile mills in creating it, main streets and town greens, transportation, education, the area's ethnic and religious groups, leisure activities, the impact of disaster, and the interaction of war and community. A final chapter deals with the region's people and politics. Its early pre-photographic history is included in the introductions to a number of chapters. Since this is a

photo book, the history we emphasize is that which spans the century and a half beginning with the invention of photography in 1839.

Selectivity also informed the choice of photographs that are included in this volume. From the outset, we recognized that our major task would be less in finding interesting and appropriate photographs than in choosing those to use. Such proved to be the case. We sorted through a wide variety of archives and private collections, looking at thousands of photos, to select the approximately three hundred that appear herein. We considered whether a picture told a story in itself or illustrated a particular point relevant to the topic of a chapter; we weighed its aesthetic quality and favored photographs which included people engaged in a variety of activities. In this manner, we tried to emphasize the human dimension of Northeast Connecticut. The reader will have the opportunity to see and judge these choices for him or herself.

In so doing, one should keep in mind the response of the famous photographer Walker Evans, when he was asked if the camera could lie. He reportedly replied, "Always." This one word answer may overstate the case. However, the reader should recognize that a photograph isn't always "pure." One compiler of a historical portrait of New York noted, "we often lose sight of a simple but important truth: that a picture of something is not the thing itself, but somebody's way of looking at it." Editors of a Chicago photo-

graphic history, likewise, remarked, "The finger that snaps the shutter may also write a message or grind an ax." This should be borne in mind when "reading" the photographs in this book. Moreover, you, the reader, will bring your own interpretation to a photo, which already has been interpreted by us. Hence, this volume may offer several levels of meaning for the history of Northeast Connecticut.

We have chosen to define that region by the twenty-eight towns that lay within the boundaries of Tolland and Windham counties and have included at least one picture from each community.* Again, such a definition points to another aspect of selectivity by the authors. While each of these towns has its own history and identity, we believe together they reflect the distinct regional characteristics imprinted by the area's mills and meadows.

Bruce M. Stave and
Michele Palmer
The Center for Oral History
The University of Connecticut
Storrs, Connecticut
Fall 1990

---

* The twenty-eight towns are: Andover, Ashford, Bolton, Brooklyn, Canterbury, Chaplin, Columbia, Coventry, Eastford, Ellington, Hampton, Hebron, Killingly, Mansfield, Plainfield, Pomfret, Putnam, Scotland, Somers, Stafford, Sterling, Thompson, Tolland, Union, Vernon, Willington, Windham, and Woodstock.

ACKNOWLEDGMENT

T he authors gratefully acknowledge the following individuals and organizatio who contributed their time, talents, and treasured pictures to this pictorial history of Northeas Connecticut. First and foremost, we wish to thank Lucy B. Crosbi publisher of the Willimantic Chronicle, without whose suppo and deep interest, this book wou not have been possible. Despite her own demanding schedule, Lucy undertook the research and writing of captions for over fifty photographs from her personal collection, and generously provided assistance and encouragement throughout the nearly two years it took to complete this project.

Special thanks also to Laura Knott Twine, founder and executive director of the Windham Textile and History Museum, for sharing her resources, her enthus asm, and her knowledge of the area's mills—from the big pictur to the tiny detail.

We are indebted to the Univer sity of Connecticut's Research Foundation and its director, Thomas Giolas, for funding the work of a research assistant, and to Mark Murphy, for his invaluable research and assistance.

The following deserve special mention for sharing their special collections with us: Rand Jimersc and the staff of Historical Manuscripts and Archives, University Connecticut Library, for material from the University of Connecticut Photograph Collection and The Wauregan and Quinebaug Company Records; Richard Schimmelpfeng and the staff of Special Collections, University of Connecticut Library; Vivian Shortreed and the staff of the Quinebaug Valley Community

Professor H. L. Garrigus used an early home-movie camera to take pictures of the Block and Bridle Show at the University of Connecticut in 1939. Garrigus taught animal husbandry at the university's College of Agriculture. The Block and Bridle Show is still an annual event at the university.
Courtesy of Kaye Andrus

Quinebaug Valley Community College Library, for the "People at Work" and "People at Play" photographs; Mark Jones and Ted Wohlson at the State Archives, Connecticut State Library, for photographs from Connecticut Cities and Towns, and the Clark Collection; Christopher Bickford and the staff of the Connecticut Historical Society; and Barbara Tucker, director of the Center for Connecticut Studies, and Kenneth Moorhead, archivist, of Eastern Connecticut State University. Photographs attributed to the Center for Oral History were from an exhibit on Willimantic developed by Daniel Schwartz, then a student at the University of Connecticut.

We offer our deep gratitude to the following individuals and representatives of local historical societies and other institutions: Roger Adams, Dirk Anderson, Faye Andrus, Sarah Axelrod, David Bartlett, Tom Beardsley, Louise Blaney, Walter Bradway, Elizabeth Brass, Alice Biesiadecki, Donna Bourque, Charlene Perkins Brown, Lynn Brown, Arnold Carlson, Bruce Clouette, Ruth Converse, Hildy Cummings, Elaine Dauphinais, Carol Davidge, Jeanne DeBell, Linda Kate Edgerton, Marion Emmons, Rudy Favretti, Arthur W. Feil, Lisa Ferriere, Carolyn Gaines, Francois Gamache, Gretchen Garner, Edward Gerry, Aimee Glaude, Rev. Roland Glaude, Dee Goslin, Marjorie Gould, Arlene Gray, Col. David Gregory, Mary Harper, Mr. and Mrs. Raymond J. Horowitz, Judith Jackson, Edward Jezierski, Barbara Jordan, Jane Knox, Kazimiera Kozlowski, Elaine Lachapelle, Rosilda Lash, Eugene Lewis, Liang Hua, Mary Carol

MacKenzie, Jean McArthur, Arland Meade, Barbara Metsack, Robert E. Miller, Arlene Mirsky, Roger Morgan, Mary G. Page, Barbara Palmer, Tim Parker, John Parson, Tony Philpotts, Dagmar Noll, Ruth Ridgeway, Ethel Robert, Pam Sadler, Rev. William Saunders, Arline Seaforth, Sue Seaver, Roberta Smith, Ruth Smith, Harvey Spink, Stanley Sumner, Susan Symonds, Irving Tannenbaum, SGM Oscar Ward, Isabel Weigold, Jeanine Upson, and David Yutzey.

For their graciousness in providing extraordinary research and assistance, as well as images, we especially want to thank S. Ardis Abbott of the Vernon Historical Society, Robert J. Miller of the Aspinock Historical Society of Putnam, Isabell Zabilansky of the Stafford Historical Society, and Walter L. Harper, professor emeritus of the University of Connecticut. We also wish to thank James A. Atwood III for candidly sharing with us his personal recollections of Wauregan Mills.

Two additional notes of thanks: First, to Roland Laramie of Laramie Photography, and to William Breadheft, director of the University of Connecticut's Photographic Services, and his entire staff, including S. Robert Pugliese, for reproducing hundreds of photographs remarkably well despite the sometimes less-than-perfect condition of the originals, and to Shelley Maloney for keeping her sense of humor and sustaining ours. Secondly, to our spouses, Sondra Astor Stave and Michael Palmer, for being understanding and helpful beyond the call of duty.

We regret if we inadvertently have omitted any individual or institution who assisted us. The cooperation of so many was essential to the completion of this book. We also accept responsibility for any errors or misjudgments which may appear within.

Finally, we wish to acknowledge all the photographers whose pictures we have used. Many of them remain anonymous, although we can mention a few names. John Prior of Moosup and George Nash of Danielson were amateurs whose skill rivaled that of professionals in the early glass-plate negative days. During that same golden age of photography at the turn of the century, there were many professionals, including Julian Beville of Willimantic, C. L. Coombs of Coventry, and Edward Rollins of Woodstock. In the 1920s, James Lees Furness built his own camera, which he used to take numerous scenes of Stafford. John McDonald of Willimantic documented the disastrous floods and hurricane of 1938, and sold his pictures of a collapsing church steeple to *Life Magazine*. In the 1970s, Lee Jacobus, with a grant from the Connecticut Commission on the Arts and a matching grant from the University of Connecticut Research Foundation, photographed the farms and mill villages of the area in the documentary manner of Walker Evans. Newspaper photographers Fran Funk and Harold Hanka captured the candid moments of more recent times. To all these, and countless others, we express our delight in presenting your outstanding images of Northeast Connecticut.

This bucolic scene took place in Pomfret in 1905. While farming was a satisfying way of life for many residents of Northeast Connecticut, it was still strenuous, labor-intensive work, besides being dependent on the weather. Haying required many hands and sunny weather for both harvesting and drying.
Courtesy of Quinebaug Valley Community College Library and Connecticut State Library Postcard Collection

In an urban and suburban state within an urban and suburban nation, Northeast Connecticut remains to this day a rural region. Not everyone is a farmer; in fact, very few residents are. However, while only one-fifth of the state was classified rural, 65 percent of Windham County and 59 percent of Tolland was so designated during the 1980s. The rolling hills of the northeast corner suited more than the growing of rocks.

Dairy and poultry farms and, at one time, tobacco planting, small-town life and natural beauty vied with the man-made landscape of the area's textile mills. As development increasingly touched the lives of area residents, one Coventry resident described the attraction of the region by lauding its virtues of community, privacy, and security. He went on to remark, "Now I'm not saying the urban environment ought not to exist . . . My mother, for instance, she dies in anything but an urban environment. When she last came to visit . . . she was kept awake by the crickets." While visitors may have to contend with the sounds of nature, few longtime dwellers in the quiet corner lose much sleep over the crickets, or the birds, or the chickens, or the cows, or the hogs. For many, nature's attractions serve as a magnet drawing them to Northeast Connecticut.

From the very beginning, our nation, following the lead of Thomas Jefferson, has celebrated the yeoman farmer, the alleged sturdy independent soul who tilled the land and made our country great. This view did not escape one observer of the area writing sixty years ago. Pliny LeRoy Harwood told his readers that "On small rocky hillside farms there has developed a race of people whose conservative habits, sturdy independence, and consistent thrift, exemplify the best qualities of the type of citizens who are 'mainstays of the Republic'." While such description tends toward cliche and reinforces a view of the "land of steady habits" that exaggerates Yankee characteristics, Northeast Connecticut's early farmers did have to work extremely hard and demonstrate ingenuity in tilling the rugged countryside.

Early farm life was plain and frugal and luxuries rare. Farmhouses stood unpainted and within them, estate inventories, such as those taken in Willington, revealed few personal possessions—"a Bible, a musket, a looking glass, a pew in the meeting house, and perhaps a pair of pewter candlesticks."
Hardscrabble life made farming for self-sufficiency more important than farming for far-off markets, which poor roads made difficult in any event. Livestock raising quickly developed as more profitable than raising grain. The poor soil required that a family of five or six be sustained on sixty to ninety acres of land. As a consequence, in the estimate of Ronald Demers, Willington had reached its maximum agricultural potential by 1800. Its young had to look elsewhere for opportunity, but many chose to stay behind. As in other parts of rural New England residents of the northeastern corner found their communities to be stable, if sometimes uneventful.

As the nineteenth century progressed, self-sufficiency grew less necessary with improvement in transportation. In Somers, the period between the Civil War and World War I witnessed prosperity. Tobacco growing revived after a hiatus during the first part of the century. However, as opposed to earlier crops, this tobacco was broadleaf, used for cigar wrapping and destined to be a trademark of the Connecticut River Valley. Lumber from the town increasingly went into the making of rail ties for the growing network of railroads. The dairy industry became highly specialized as citizens of Hartford and Springfield no longer kept their own cows or grew their own fruit and vegetables. In 1888, several of Somers' farmers and businessmen established the Somers Creamery Company, later absorbed into H. P. Hood and Company. They successfully organized the local milk industry and marketed its roduct. Fruit and vegetable growers also took advantage of new technology and marketing techniques.

On one Ellington farm started in the very early nineteenth century, milking and caring for the cows, raising their feed—corn and hay—and helping with the horses and oxen initially was all done by hand. By the early 1900s, farmers increasingly employed machines; the mowing machine, the corn harvester, the ensilage cutter all came into use. The electric milker emerged around the end of World War I as electricity became more common. Machinery allowed for increased tobacco production, but by the

1950s, with the development of tobacco leaf "homogenization," raising of the crop ended.

In that town, as in a number of other communities in eastern Connecticut, several of the farmers originally settled under the auspices of the Jewish Agricultural Society, which took part in a worldwide effort to settle Jewish immigrants on the land. Baron Maurice de Hirsch and his wife had endowed the Jewish Colonization Association, which in turn made low interest loans to settlers. This money seeded initial installments on Ellington farms as it did in Columbia and Hebron and on farms throughout the world. The sometimes inexperienced farmers

received guidance in agriculture from the JAS and in 1905, they helped organize the Connecticut Jewish Farmers Association. Such farmers, as well as others, played a leading role in dairy and poultry production throughout the state.

By the second half of the twentieth century, successful dairies such as Bradway Farm in Union reflected consolidation of resources. Bradway Farm dated from the late nineteenth century and merged two separate farms which existed prior to 1890. Initially, it raised dairy products, vegetables, and livestock. In the early 1900s, the Bradways increased their herd of cows to twenty. First they sold only cream,

he camaraderie of farming is evident in the faces of this Phoenixville group in 1912. Farmer Frederick Bennett, his daughter Mildred, and other workers are holding scythes, rakes, and forks for haying. Women may look unusual in a farming scene, but in fact weren't. They labored in the fields alongside the men, in addition to being responsible for household work. One of the reasons for the mills' success was that young women—those not as enthralled with farm life as Mildred Bennett—were seeking a way to escape the farm. For many, though, it turned out to be exchanging one kind of drudgery for another.
Courtesy of Quinebaug Valley Community College Library

John Prior, an amateur photographer from Plainfield, photographed many farm scenes, specializing in quiet moments like this elderly man shucking corn in a barn, circa 1910. Everyone worked on the farm, including women, children, and old people. The latter were expected to work as long as they were able, doing chores like shucking corn, sharpening tools, and tending animals.
Courtesy of Quinebaug Valley Community College Library

then calves, and then milk to the Connecticut Milk Producers Association. To supplement his income, the original owner's son, who worked with his father, took a second job at a local sawmill. As a consequence, soon the farm was selling lumber, cordwood, and railroad ties.

During the 1920s a number of machines came into use, which facilitated haying. Other improvements occurred and when the original owner's grandson took over in 1958, the cow herd had grown to 40. Ten years later, it was 100 and when the great grandson joined his father as an operator of the farm, it became necessary to hire workers from outside of the family. Within a few years, the farm incorporated with a milking herd of more than 250 and a total herd of 500. By the early 1980s, the farm ranked in the top ten in size in the state and the herd ranked first in Tolland County in milk production and butterfat. Not unlike industry and corporations elsewhere, Bradway Farm aimed for, and achieved, efficiency. In 1983, total milk production amounted to 8,308,000 pounds; per man that came to 1,039,000 pounds, more than twice the national average.

Today, fewer farms in America feed more people than ever before. In the westernmost corner of Tolland County in tiny Union, Bradway Farm illustrated this fact with vigor. Only one worker did the milking as the cows were brought to a milking parlor in three shifts—11:00 a.m., 6:30 p.m., and 2:30 a.m. Given the number of cows by 1990, milking occurred almost twenty-four hours per day. The milking herd had increased to 375 and the entire herd totaled 700. Each cow produced 22,700 pounds of milk and 844 of butterfat. Only six workers plus three or four family members operated the

...rm. The modern age did not escape the farms of Northeast Connecticut, although in most instances, unlike the Bradway's enterprise which grew, the small family farm faded into the past.

The number of acres farmed in Connecticut diminished from 591,000 in 1982 to 464,000 in 1987 and one authority estimated an annual 2 percent decrease since then. However, as farming became endangered, the popularity of country fairs continued. In 1990, fifty-five were scheduled throughout the state, giving urban, suburban, and small-town dwellers an opportunity to make an acquaintance with the once predominant agriculture. From jam judging to oxen pulls, people who never milked a cow in their lives delighted in the rural past. Just as farmers of earlier times sought the essence of community in agricultural societies and organizations like the Grange, modern folks in fits of nostalgia looked to the country fair for comfort in a complex world.

While many have ceased to operate in the region, the northeastern corner witnessed the birth of a number of successful fairs. As early as 1809, Pomfret, Woodstock, and Brooklyn founded the Pomfret United Agricultural Society, the first Agricultural Society formed in the state; in 1820, the name changed to the Windham County Agricultural Society. The group held fairs alternately in Pomfret and Woodstock. Farmers won awards for the fastest plowing and for the quality of their livestock. The community gathered as participants and spectators, and a fine time was had by all. In 1852, the fair moved to Brooklyn; in 1859, Woodstock held its own. For ten cents admission, one cold see fruits and flowers exhibited in the vestry of the Baptist Church; pens held cattle nearby; trotting and carriage horses could be found under the elms.

In the western part of the region, the Tolland County Agricultural Fair had its roots in 1853 when a group of citizens organized an agricultural society. The next year, visitors to the fair saw a cattle show on the first day and an exhibit of horses and colts and a plowing match on the second; trotting horses raced the next year up and down Tolland Street; subsequently, the Agricultural Society built a fenced-in fair grounds with a graded half-mile racetrack. Rockville rather than Tolland later emerged as the central fair area. Earlier, during the winter of 1838-39, farmers in Somers held a contest to see which of the town's school districts could show the largest group of oxen and steers. They yoked up 210 pairs of cattle and exhibited them at Somers Street. The interest and enthusiasm for this event gave rise to the Four Town Fair, which involved Somers, Enfield, Ellington, and East Windsor and for a long time rotated among the towns. By the beginning of the twentieth century, footraces, jumping contests, dancing, and baseball games between the towns became part of the program. In 1906, a wheel of fortune and other games of chance could be counted among the fair's distractions. Part agricultural show, part carnival, such fairs moved through the twentieth century.

Today's Stafford Motor Speedway stands at the Stafford fairgrounds, which dates back to 1870 and the few Stafford citizens who raised about four hundred dollars as partial payment for the site. Trotting developed as one of the most notable features of the Stafford Fair and the sport attracted spectators from far and wide including Connecticut's governors, who usually visited on the fair's second day. After World War II, in 1948, the fair's owner, Clarence Benton, introduced auto racing to the fairgrounds; however, until about 1955, sulky racing continued to be the main draw. Afterwards, the roar of engines belonging to midget autos and stock cars silenced the neighs of horses. By 1969, the fair had run its course. New speeds and new technology supplanted a rural pastime.

Despite such change, the northeastern corner retains much of its pastoral charm. The towns of Tolland and Windham counties continue to provide a large chunk of Connecticut's countryside.

21

Oxen were the standard beasts of burden on farms in Northeast Connecticut. One or two pairs, like Andover farmer George Stanley's oxen pictured here, circa 1902, was typical, although one Tolland farmer used five pairs of oxen for hauling logs to a Rockville sawmill, a sight that stopped onlookers along the way. Some farmers used oxen for plowing, but others, especially younger ones, preferred horses, which were faster than the slow but steady oxen.
Courtesy of Andover Historical Society

Fixing a fence is an essential chore on dairy farms like Murdoch's Farm in Pomfret. Many farms in Northeast Connecticut are dairy farms, although at one time chicken farming was more prevalent. This 1975 photograph is not just a document of farm work, but an interesting character study of workers Jimmy Davis and William Schuller.
Lee Jacobus photograph; courtesy of the photographer

The lone woman in the background attests to the isolation of this farmhouse and barn in Stafford in the early 1900s. The area of most Northeast Connecticut farms was under fifty acres, which was relatively small, but still large enough to keep farmers at a considerable distance from one another.
Courtesy of Stafford Historical Society

This scene of a farm family in Brooklyn, shows the isolation and poverty that accompanied some farmers' struggle to eke out a living from the land. With farming also extremely sensitive to economic recession, it's no wonder that so many area farmers moved west or switched to mill or factory work.
Courtesy of State Archives, Connecticut State Library

Many farms stayed in the same family for years, such as the Hevey farm in Hampton, shown here in the 1890s with several generations living and working together.
Courtesy of Connecticut Historical Society

E. D. Harbeck's Cash Store in Danielson was a new concept in the 1890s. Until then, many country stores used bartering or trading in exchange for goods, with very little cash ever being handled. Storekeepe[rs] often brought their goods directly to the farmer. They then took farm produce in trade, hauling it to Providence with ox teams and exchangin[g] it once again for more goods. Country stores usually carried a wide variety of merchandise, although Harbeck's seems to concentrate on clothing, including hats and caps, boots and shoes.
Courtesy of State Archives, Connecticut State Library

Cutting ice from rivers, lakes, and millponds was a wintertime occupation for farmers in the days before refrigerators. The work had to be done quickly, before a thaw or before the ice got too thick to cut. After it was harvested, it was stored in tall sheds, or icehouses. Because of the great density of the ice—about a foot thick—it kept until the following summer, and sometimes until it was harvested again. The ice-cutting scenes here are on the Quinebaug River in Putnam, circa 1885, and on an Oneco mill pond in 1915.
Courtesy of Aspinock Historical Society of Putnam

Courtesy of Quinebaug Valley Community College Library

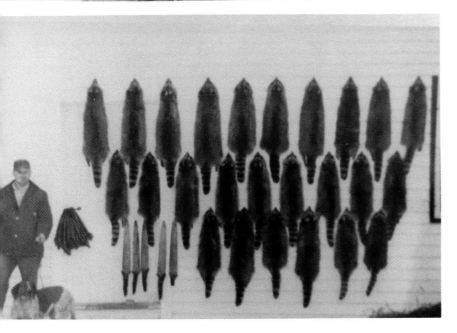

Harvey Spink of Eastford stands next to his raccoon and mink pelts, circa 1935. Hunting was a lucrative sideline for some residents of rural Northeast Connecticut. Raccoons brought ten to twelve dollars apiece, and minks were worth twenty-five dollars, more than a day's wages in a mill. Some men would set their traps before leaving in the morning and check on them upon returning home at night. Others worked at trapping full time in the fall and winter.
Courtesy of Harvey Spink

25

Boiling down maple syrup is an early spring tradition in rural Northeast Connecticut. In this 1975 photograph, Ed Rufleth of Canterbury was practicing this ancient art with a mixture of old makeshift arrangements and new accoutrements, such as the brand-new galvanized can behind him.
Lee Jacobus photograph; courtesy of the photographer

The haystacks of E. C. Pinney of Stafford stand in neat rows in this peaceful farm scene. The cotton cloths covering the hay were made by the Ladies of the Universalist Church. Although water-repellent canvas was sometimes used to keep the hay dry, these dainty squares seem more like decorative doilies.
Courtesy of Stafford Historical Society

The Great Wall of Sterling, located in the village of Oneco, stretches along Pine Hill Road No. 1 for almost eight hundred feet. Begun during the Civil War, the wall was constructed out of waste stone from a local quarry. Master stonemason Henry Sayles, a Sterling resident and descendant of Roger Williams, supervised the massive force of men and horses that labored twenty years to complete the wall. The wall was built in two sections with a gap of thirteen feet in between to allow animals or machinery to pass through. It is six feet at its highest point and up to eleven feet in width.
Lee Jacobus photograph; courtesy of the photographer

Sulky racing was the highlight of the
Stafford Fair, attended by both local
farmers and well-to-do guests from the
nearby Stafford Springs Hotel. Almost
from the fair's beginnings in 1870,
some of the best horses and drivers in
the East competed here, and the track
had to be enlarged several times as the
popularity of the sport grew. The fair
also featured a midway, fireworks,
livestock shows, and agricultural
displays, but sulky racing continued to
be the main attraction, even after auto
racing was introduced. Eventually,
however, the Stafford Motor Speedway
superseded the horse races and even the
fair itself. By 1969, the nearly one-
hundred-year-old tradition of the
Stafford Fair had come to an end.
Courtesy of Stafford Historical Society

At the midway of the Willimantic Agricultural Fair in Horseshoe Park, shown here in 1907, you could have your fortune told by gypsies, who migrated to Willimantic every year, living in camps, as they made the rounds of local fairs. There was also a large exhibition hall, a bandstand, a vaudeville stage and an 1,800-seat grandstand for viewing trotting races. The fair ended in 1913 when the American Thread Company, who owned the land, decided to turn it into a Recreation Park for its employees. Starting in 1914, annual fairs were held each fall until 1952 at the Elks Fairgrounds. Courtesy of Lucy B. Crosbie and the Willimantic Chronicle

Autumn in Northeast Connecticut still means country fair time in many towns, carrying on a tradition that began in 1852 with the Brooklyn Fair, the nation's oldest continuous agricultural fair. These pictures, taken by Harold Hanka during the 1970s, show cattle vying at the Hebron Fair, pigs battling in a beauty contest at the Woodstock Fair, and men sitting on a tractor enjoying the sights at the Chaplin Fair.

Harold Hanka photographs; courtesy of the photographer

The rhythmic patterns of this collapsed barn in Putnam, "like waves in the sea, slowly changing shape," captured the imagination of the photographer. According to him, he was "catching an instant in visual time that would never exist again." Indeed, the rapidly changing landscape of Northeast Connecticut will never exist again. Housing developments and shopping malls have already changed the look of the landscape in other areas of the region. There are still farms of course, with barns in good repair, but their numbers have continued to decline.
Lee Jacobus photograph; courtesy of the photographer

...e of the most enduring farms in Northeast Connecticut is at the ...versity of Connecticut's School of Agriculture. The horse barns ... farmhouse are seen in this view of Horsebarn Hill, a popular ...e for sledding in the winter. Many generations of children have ...ed the horses, cows, and sheep at the farm and eaten ice cream at ...nearby Dairy Bar.
...ices L. Funk photograph; courtesy of the photographer

Chapter Two
MILLS: THE MAN-MADE LANDSCAPE

The age of the workers in the spinning room of the Grosvenor Dale Mills in 1890 is striking—most of them are teenagers or younger. Many started at age eleven or twelve, standing on boxes if necessary to reach the machines. Children's wages were lower than adults, but were still considered an essential contribution to the family income. Courtesy of Thompson Historical Society

Imagine Northeast Connecticut without its mills, if you can. Much of the area's man-made landscape would disappear as the warp and woof of the region's mill buildings unwind stone by stone in the mind's eye. The development of the mill towns of Tolland and Windham counties owe much to these edifices in which the craft of textile manufacture was successfully merchanized and the industrial revolution brought to America. From Rockville to Willimantic to Wauregan to Danielson, Putnam and the Grosvenordales, wherever waterpower, machinery, labor, and capital could be brought together, the textile mills left their impact upon the land and its people.

This impact sometimes meant waves of migrants seeking work; it meant prosperity and a better living; at other times it brought poor working conditions and a feeling of exploitation. It bound management and workers together in a spirit of harmony and community; it spelled class antagonism and bitter strikes. It bred optimism and a sense of progress; on the other hand, just as the mills were in the vanguard of industrialization, their departure, first to the south and then abroad, marked the onset of de-industrialization and concern for the area's future. Above all, they demonstrated how changes in the organization of work affect the development of society.

For the mill and the factory or "manufactory," as it was once called, emerged as a new way to organize work. First on a small scale, then on a grander one, work changed from that done in small groups to that done in larger ones. When Samuel Slater joined with William Almy and Smith Brown to establish the first waterpowered cotton mill in Pawtucket, Rhode Island, in December 1790, the effect on Connecticut was not far behind. Manchester served as the site of the state's first cotton mill in 1794, although more than two decades earlier in 1770, mechanized textile production began in the town of Scotland with the first wool-carding machine built in the English colonies. By the end of the eighteenth century, the system that would spread to Northeast Connecticut and be modified and enlarged had been set—small riverside mills, Awkwright spinning frames, child labor, plain and crowded housing, and a company store.

In Willimantic, the early nineteenth century mills of Perez Richmond and the Jillson family, laid the foundation for what would later come. The story of that city's main industry offers a useful case study for the entire Northeast Connecticut region. In 1854, Austin Dunham and partners organized the Willimantic Linen Company to produce linen goods. However, the Crimean War limited the supply of flax needed for linen production and the company converted to the manufacturing of cotton thread by the end of the 1850s. Its first plant consisted of an old cotton mill, called the Spool Shop, built by the Jillsons in 1825 and another nearby wooden mill. The company also owned and operated a small mill in South Willington, which discontinued when its machinery and operatives were transferred to the permanent No. Mill, which opened in Willimantic in 1861, the first year of the Civil War. Expanding business during wartime encouraged the construction of Mill No. 2, built of stone dug from the local river bed.

By 1884, through acquisition of other property and the building the No. 4 mill, the Willimantic Linen Company stood as an impressively complex operation. No. 4 served as a model for cotton mills worldwide; its ground floor held the record as longest, 820 feet long by 174 feet wide. The company, however, developed more than mill buildings. As early as 1865, it had built workers' housing when the New Village tenements were constructed. Twenty years later, The Oaks section added additional mill housing, but this time individual cottages rather than multiple housing were the order of the day. In addition, wh today the Windham Textile and istory Museum at the junction Union and Main streets, was ied as the company general store ith the top floor serving as the unham Hall Library for em- oyees.

The housing, the library, the ore, the general working condi- ins led one observer in 1885 to ie, perhaps much too uncritically, e Willimantic experience as an ample of "benevolent" mill vning. Writing for *Harper's*, aniel Pidgeon, who was very tronizing of the workers, par- cularly the Irish immigrants, marked, "Certainly, if there is ie establishment which, more an any other in America, encour- es hope for the future of labor, it the Willimantic Thread Com- ny of Connecticut." He de- ribed No. 4 mill as spotlessly ean and remarked how young omen, fifteen to twenty-five ars of age, stood by the spinning ames, "All of them are neatly ressed, and wear a uniform white ien apron of tasteful cut, while eir faces are clean, bright, and ealthful, and their hair carefully, ten skilfully [*sic*], dressed." The ene may have been posed with ual care and skill by the com- ny (see photograph within).

Pidgeon attributed much of the mill's benevolence to the leader- ship of Colonel Barrows, the president and manager of the company, who joined it in 1874 and became general manager in 1876. Like many other mill bosses of his day, Barrows expressed a strong paternalism as evidenced by his comment, "This mill and these people are my life, my career, the next greatest responsi- bility I have in the world after that of my own family. I dare as soon desert my flag in action as leave my hands without their natural and appointed head." In accord with the Social Darwinism of the day, the philosophy of survival of the fittest, he was that "natural and appointed head."

By 1892, two thousand employ- ees worked at American Thread and their annual production was over fifteen million miles of thread and yarn. Men like Bar- rows, then, saw themselves as father figures for the toiling masses. At Wauregan, James Atwood left a similar stamp on his "model community." As one contemporary observed, no intoxicating liquors were sold in Wauregan and "great pains (were) taken to promote the best interests of the operatives and residents." Paternalism ruled.

This 1855 lithograph of Rockville, published by a Hartford printer, shows three mills, all with bell towers. They are from left to right: Leed's Mill, Rock Mill, and American Mill. Because of thirteen separate falls in the Hockanum River as it passes through Rockville, a succession of mills formed along the river, making the town more diversified than many one-company towns. The river's unusually pure water was ideally suited for fine wool processing and Rockville gained a national reputation for producing the finest quality woolens and worsteds. Courtesy of Vernon Historical Society

The same view of Rockville was taken in this circa 1870 photograph. The Rock Mill, in the foreground, begun in 1821, was the first large woolen mill in Rockville. The tenter racks, on which wool was stretched and dried, are visible in the lower right-hand corner of the photo. The Second Congrega- tional Church in the center seems to be watching over the activities of the mills below it. Courtesy of Vernon Historical Society

Some workers accepted this rule; others did not. In the same year that America entered the Spanish-American War, 1898, Willimantic Linen became part of American Thread, joining mills in Maine, Massachusetts, and Rhode Island to form a network of five. American Thread would dominate Willimantic life and culture from the turn of the century. As one worker commented, "The American Thread was the big industry . . . When I was young that was practically the only place you could get a job." There were other small mills and businesses, but that one employer dominated. As the twentieth century progressed, any sense that the mill was "like a family" became diluted and labor strife intensified. A cut in wages or layoffs at such a dominant employer vibrated through the entire community.

In 1925, a 10 percent wage cut led to a strike that would last for over twenty-four weeks and divide the community. On its third day, March 12, the mill's general agent, Don H. Curtis, announced that the huge complex would remain open "to all who seek work as well as (to) the striking operatives." A schoolgirl of the time remembered many years later that workers marched up and down the streets and police with drawn guns patrolled the area. The company brought young girls from Maine to work the mills—"Scabs we used to call them." Before the strike ended in September 1925, workers were evicted from their homes and the community had become polarized, leaving wounds which lasted long after their making. (See photographs within.)

Nine years later, workers in Putnam and Danielson joined others in the state as part of a national textile strike; National Guard troops with fixed bayonets stood at the ready. In Putnam, four hundred workers of the Belding-Heminway-Corticelli Silk Company left the plant under the protection of a phalanx of Guardsmen, while a crowd of three thousand howled in anger at the troops and the emerging workers; a machine gun unit mobilized at the State Armory; in Willimantic, clergymen counseled their parishioners to refrain from violence. By this time, then, a rift slashed through the sense of "family" expressed many years earlier by Colonel Barrows at the Willimantic Linen Company. Some workers probably did share this feeling and nostalgia reinforces it as years go by and former textile workers remember their working past. However, by the end of the Depression decade, m[] workers stood a world apart from their counterparts of a half-century earlier, although many continuities still existed.

The needs of World War II infused new energy into the mill[] of Northeast Connecticut. Army-Navy contracts meant more business for American Thread in 1943, but with victory and the conclusion of the war the handwriting was on the mill wall. The company moved equipment to Georgia in 1948 and in 1950 American Thread's Fall River plant closed. Two years later, it built a plant in South Carolina which would be followed a doze[] years after by one in North Carolina. In 1980, when the company announced its decision to move its polyester thread wor[] from Willimantic to a Southern plant, rumor flowed that the entire plant would soon be close[]

Drawings of mills, such as the Willimantic Linen Company (later American Thread Company), circa 1878, were usually commissioned by the management, and emphasized their neat orderliness and benign domination of the surrounding landscape, even an urban setting. Their bell towers were visibl[] from afar, like church steeples, and the bells themselves defined the rhythm of daily life. There was order, stability, and the promise o[] regular employment in these solid-looking buildings. The railroad contributed to the flourishing of the mills, as did the smokestacks, which indicated the change from waterpower to steam power. The latter, however, were an ironic foreshadowing of the ultimate success of steam-powered mills in the South.
Courtesy of Francois Gamache

One thousand workers were still employed and the general manager said the company was making every effort to keep the plant in Willimantic by keeping the company productive. Within five years, such optimism had to confront a complete shut down.

As with so many other New England textile mills, the longest continuing plant in Northeast Connecticut moved south. Now, empty shells marked the man-made landscape, although creative townspeople and developers throughout the area search for worthwhile readaptive uses. Where mills once stood, shops and housing may be substituted. The special mill architecture of Northeast Connecticut perseveres giving the region its distinctive character. Buildings alone, however, are not enough to determine this character. The people who worked in the mills and their descendants, women and men, Yankees and immigrants, from mainland or Puerto Rican island, wove not merely fabric but the texture of community life.

The bell in the North Tower of Wauregan Mills No. 1 rang every hour until the advent of the steam whistle. The picket fence which set off the property was painted white every year to provide a bucolic atmosphere. A village maintenance crew of forty individuals cared for the mill village.
Courtesy of Historical Manuscripts and Archives, University of Connecticut Library

The tranquil river, fully blossomed trees, and gracefully arched bridge nearly obscure the Windham Manufacturing Company just beyond them. An idealized view of mills was a common theme of turn-of-the-century photographs and paintings, which often tried to block out some of the harsher realities of mill life. Windham Manufacturing Company was a cotton mill, located on Bridge Street in Willimantic, along with several other small silk and cotton mills.
Courtesy of Walter L. Harper

An aerial view of the Wauregan Mills compound taken in the mid-1940s shows a landscape unchanged since the late nineteenth century. Mills were often built in isolated areas of Northeast Connecticut where land and water rights were cheap. They were also located near rivers (in this case, the Quinebaug River) to make use of the abundant waterpower. Prior to construction of Wauregan Mills, no town existed on this site. The entire community was constructed by the mill owners, including the church and parsonage in the foreground. By maintaining the rural character of the area, mill owners attempted to soften the impact of industrialism. As time went on, however, they were not always successful. Courtesy of Historical Manuscripts and Archives, University of Connecticut Library

The U.S. Thread Company Mills, Willimantic *is one of several local mill scenes painted by J. Alden Weir, American impressionist and summer resident of Windham Center. The painting must have been named retrospectively by Weir, or someone else, since he painted the scene sometime between 1893 and 1897, when the mill was still the Willimantic Linen Company. It wasn't until 1898 that it became the American (not U.S.) Thread Company. In any case, Weir's romanticized vision is similar to scenes by French Impressionists, like Monet, who also painted industrial buildings and smokestacks nestled in a peaceful landscape. Weir, who died in 1919, is buried in the Windham Center Cemetery. His home in Branchville, in western Connecticut, is now a national park.*
Collection of Mr. and Mrs. Raymond J. Horowitz; partial and promised gift to National Gallery of Art

In reality, the mills of Northeast Connecticut were not as idyllic as the myth perpetuated by some artists and photographers. This 1967 aerial view of the twenty-acre American Thread Company shows its sprawling sixteen-building complex. The gigantic Mill No. 4, in the background, was the largest one-story thread mill in the world when it was built in 1884. Although a succession of developers have owned the buildings since the company moved south in 1985, most of the buildings are still vacant. Courtesy of Lucy B. Crosbie and the Willimantic Chronicle

Mill-sponsored group photographs of employees are almost always outdoors, with the mill as a backdrop. The unspoken message is that the solidness of the mill is literally backing up its employees. This group has been tentatively identified as Wauregan weavers from the 1890s. Courtesy of Historical Manuscripts and Archives, University of Connecticut Library

The entire mill building is included in this 1890 photograph of Manhasset Company workers, not just as background but as a central feature of the photograph. While all the workers are assembled in front of the building, the long distance shot minimizes their individualism and importance. The Putnam mill manufactured cotton fabric for tire cores. The small building in front of the mill was the paymaster's office. Courtesy of Aspinock Historical Society of Putnam

Mill owners often commissioned photographs of their workers to foster a feeling of togetherness and pride. Copies of the photographs were either given to the employees or made available for sale. In this 1888 picture, however, the subject is the photographer taking the photograph. The workers are from the Putnam Woolen Company, built in 1842 on the site of the first cotton mill in Windham County. Courtesy of Aspinock Historical Society of Putnam

These employees of the Aldrich Manufacturing Company in Moosup can be identified as mill overseers by their vests, ties, and pocket watches, symbols of middle management in the late nineteenth century. William Hutchins (top row, left) was overseer of the cloth room. The names of the other overseers are not known, but they would be in charge of carding, spinning, weaving, and other mill operations. Overseers kept long hours, often being first to arrive in the morning and last to leave at night, as a check on operations in the mill. Courtesy of Quinebaug Valley Community College Library

This 1920 photograph of American Thread Company managers shows company agent, David Moxon (third from left in front row). The mill agent was overseer of the entire mill operation, with dictatorial control over workers and policies. In the nineteenth century, an agent's home was typically an elegant mansion that sat on a hill literally overseeing the mill. A few agents, such as James S. Atwood of Wauregan Mills, and E. Burton Shaw of the American Thread Company, eventually assumed ownership of the company, but most were managers who ran the day-to-day business of the mill for its absentee owners. Courtesy of Center for Oral History, University of Connecticut

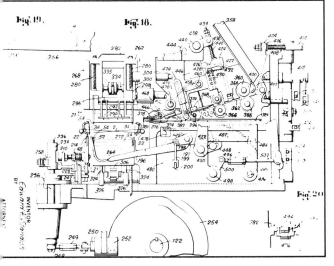

This schematic drawing for a skein-winding machine was designed by an American Thread Company employee, Edward K. Standish. It shows the intricacy of even a small machine, which was used to wind embroidery skeins. Besides the weavers, spinners, and other employees who actually produced the thread or cloth, textile mills hired designers and machinists to create, build, update, and maintain the machinery.
Courtesy of Windham Textile and History Museum

The cast-iron gears, pulleys, and chain drives needed to run the machinery at the American Thread Company were all produced on site. Items were first carved out of wood; then molds were made to accept the hot iron. The machine shown here is a tube winder used for transferring thread from a large batch to smaller measured batches.
Courtesy of Windham Textile and History Museum

In this posed photograph, circa 1890, four women thread testers at the Willimantic Linen Company are shown neatly dressed and comfortably seated amid airy surroundings, complete with well-cared-for houseplants. The plants, however, were not primarily for decorative effect, but were used to increase the humidity level of the room. Cotton mills were kept deliberately hot and humid to keep the threads from breaking. They were also noisy, oily, and dusty, conditions not at all apparent in the tea-party atmosphere of this photograph. Mills were so noisy that workers often used sign language to communicate with each other, and so dusty that photographs had to be taken without a flash, since any spark might have ignited the dust and caused a fire. *Courtesy of State Archives, Connecticut State Library*

The awesomeness of fifty thousand spindles in one place is conveyed in this 1915 photo of the spinning room at American Thread Company's Mill No. 4. About half of the thread spun was for the home market; the rest was for commercial use, sold to other textile mills who wove it into cloth. *Courtesy of Windham Textile and History Museum*

This Barber Coleman Warper was one of four such machines installed in 1944 at Wauregan Mills. It was operated by one person. If there was a short run, the end of the yarn would have to be tied by hand. Women's dexterity was helpful here, as was the fluorescent lighting which made it easier to identify the yarn. *Courtesy of Historical Manuscripts and Archives, University of Connecticut Library*

The dress is more casual, the look more candid in this photograph of two women preparing warps at the Quinebaug Company in 1901. They seem to be enjoying the short break from their work, even if it's just long enough to have their picture taken. Unlike the contrived pleasantness of the previous picture, photographer George W. Nash captured a more basic beauty inherent in the realities of mill life: the repetitive patterning of the spools, the contrasts of light and dark, and the even starker contrast between people and machines. Courtesy of Quinebaug Valley Community College Library

In the cloth room of Wauregan Mills, women workers are inspecting for imperfections in the fabric. The process is called flat fold inspection. The man in the center is either the overseer or someone bringing cloth to the women. Note that this is before fluorescent lights were installed. Sixty percent of the mill workers were women who served as weavers, spinners, and cloth inspectors because it was believed that they had more dexterity for such jobs. Men usually served as carders, mechanics, and maintainers, and ran some of the heavier equipment.
Courtesy of Historical Manuscripts and Archives, University of Connecticut Library

Of the two workers operating the slasher at Wauregan Mills, the man at the left, Mr. Duval, was the boss slasher or tender. Mill lore maintains that sometimes the size box near Mr. Duval often foamed when it filled with steam. Workers found that if they urinated into the box, the acid in their urine would kill the foam.
Courtesy of Historical Manuscripts and Archives, University of Connecticut Library

These spool shop employees at the American Thread Company in 1950 were paid by piecework—either by count or by weight—rather than by regular salary. Women's salaries in mills, as elsewhere, has inequitably been lower than men's, but being paid by piecework enabled some women to earn more than they ordinarily would by producing more, although it probably created more stress in the process. The spools they were winding were for the home sewing market. Courtesy of Windham Textile and History Museum

The main source of light for these weavers is natural daylight. Their looms, set up under windows, took advantage of the free light. The only other light source seems to be a single bare bulb above the man in the background.
Courtesy of Historical Manuscripts and Archives, University of Connecticut Library

The worker standing next to a loom is promoting its safety feature of covered shuttles, which prevented them from slipping and causing injury. Both this and the previous photo were originally identified as Wauregan Mills, but former owner James Atwood III questioned the identification, based on the differences in window configuration and interior walls.
Courtesy of Historical Manuscripts and Archives, University of Connecticut Library

The company store of the Willimantic Linen Company opened in 1877, providing employees with a convenient, if uncompetitive, place to shop. Local farmers and butchers gathered in front of the store to sell their wares several times a week. This picture was taken in the spring of 1888, just after the Great Blizzard. The building also housed a library for company workers, offices, and rooms for meetings and night school classes.
Courtesy of Windham Textile and History Museum

The Dunham Hall Library, shown here in 1896, was built for the employees of the Willimantic Linen Company as part of a cultural program that also provided courses in singing, drawing, and English. Eventually, the library was opened to the public as well, but by the 1930s the American Thread Company closed the facility, about the same time it was letting go of its housing and other non-manufacturing properties. The books were divided up among area libraries, mill employees, and local schools. The library room has since been restored as part of the Windham Textile and History Museum.
Courtesy of Windham Textile and History Museum

*he company cafeteria at Wauregan Mills was established during World War II. Management te there, as well as workers, but at different times. The cafeteria was subsidized at 40 percent of ost. It was discontinued in 1949 when management became concerned over time lost at lunch. reviously, children often brought lunch to their parents and learned to operate the machinery hile their parents ate. This practice ended in the 1930s with controls on child labor.
ourtesy of Historical Manuscripts and Archives, University of Connecticut Library*

These mill girls of the 1920s pose on the porch of the Elms Boarding
House, which was built as a residence for single women employees of
the Willimantic Linen Company in 1865. It was part of a housing
project called the New Village, directly across the street from the mill.
While residing in company housing wasn't mandatory as it was in
some other mills, there was little other choice for employees, besides
private boarding houses. Mills in the larger cities, like Willimantic,
attracted single workers, while the small-town mills encouraged
married employees with families, thus insuring a future generation of
mill workers.
Courtesy of Windham Textile and History Museum

In the South Village area of Wauregan, workers' homes built by
Wauregan Mills were one part of a huge industrial complex. The
homes were in either two or four-unit buildings, with three rooms
upstairs and three downstairs. To reside here, at least one family
member had to work in the mill. Rents were automatically deducted
from salaries. Most of the workers lived in mill-built housing, but
some came to work from the surrounding countryside.
Courtesy of Historical Manuscripts and Archives, University of
Connecticut Library

Mill housing built for skilled laborers was a step above the look-alike tenements or row houses of the unskilled. The Oaks section in Willimantic was built by the Willimantic Linen Company in 1885 for its engineers, carpenters, and other skilled laborers, and offered a choice of several architectural styles. Quercus Avenue, the main street of the development, is named after the Latin word for "oaks."
Courtesy of Center for Oral History, University of Connecticut

75% of the Purchase Price can Remain on Mortgage at 6% ON ALL DWELLINGS

ANNOUNCING THE SALE

AT PUBLIC AUCTION TO THE HIGHEST BIDDER

88 Desirable Dwelling Properties   3 Garage Properties   25 Parcels of Unimproved Land (43.5 ACRES)

THE PROPERTY OF
THE
American Thread Company
INCORPORATED
AT
WILLIMANTIC, CONN.

SATURDAY, JUNE 25, 1938, Starting at 10 A.M. (Daylight Saving Time)

THE SALE INCLUDES:
40 Cottages
40 Two Family Dwellings
8 Four Family Dwellings
3 Multi-Car Garages
25 Parcels Unimproved Land
43.5 Acres

LOCATIONS INCLUDE:
Main Street   Ives Street   Pleasant Street
Quercus Avenue   Crescent Street
Fairview Street   Factory Street

FOR FULL PARTICULARS APPLY TO

SAMUEL T. FREEMAN & CO. AUCTIONEERS
1808-10 Chestnut Street, Philadelphia   80 FEDERAL STREET, BOSTON, MASS.   27 William Street, New York
LOCAL OFFICE: ON MAIN STREET, NEAR THE MILL OFFICE. ➤ LOOK FOR THE SIGN. ◀

When the cottages of Quercus Avenue were auctioned off with all the other mill-owned housing in 1938, it was reported that many of them were bought by their original renters or other mill workers, rather than by speculators as was the case with other mill sell-outs. The cost of maintaining residential properties had proved too costly for most companies during the Depression. Moreover, after the workers' strikes, such as the one in 1925 at the American Thread Company, mill owners began to realize that they couldn't control every aspect of their workers' lives. In the same year, the Willimantic mill gave up some of its other holdings, including Recreation Park to the town, and the Armory to the state.
Courtesy of Windham Textile and History Museum

These East Brooklyn residents are posed in front of a building that once housed mill employees, but in 1975, when this photograph was taken, it was just another housing development in a former mill town. Directly across the street is Quebec Square, considered a model workers' community when it was built in the 1860s by the Quinebaug Company for its employees. When the Quinebaug Company closed in 1942, many workers stayed on, living out their retirement years in Quebec Square. The development was recently restored for use as low-cost housing.
Lee Jacobus photograph; courtesy of the photographer

Women workers marched down Willimantic's Main Street in the early days of the 1925 strike at the American Thread Company. The mill operatives sought to demonstrate their solidarity in protest of a 10 percent wage cut. Women comprised a large majority of the work force at American Thread, as they did in many textile mills in New England. The practice of using Main Street as a forum to air grievances from time to time has continued to the present day, a 1990 march by Willimantic's Latino residents showed.
Courtesy of Roger Morgan, CST Ret.

A state policeman escorts three replacement workers, called "scabs" by the strikers, onto American Thread Company grounds as a large crowd looks on. The replacements, usually from out of town, were a source of much tension. The company's decision to bring in replacements was a sign that the mill owners were determined to maintain their position on the wage cut.
Courtesy of Roger Morgan, CST Ret.

A state policeman collars a suspect during the 1925 strike at the American Thread Company. The strike began as a peaceful protest, but confrontations ensued as the strike dragged on. While the mood of the town was tense throughout the conflict, there was less violence than in the 1934 strikes in Putnam and Danielson. Incidents occurred at textile mills there as part of a nationwide strike protesting the difference between Northern and Southern textile wages.
Courtesy of Roger Morgan, CST Ret.

Striking workers at the American Thread Company pose with their families in front of "Tent City," after being evicted from company-owned housing in June 1925. The strikers erected fifteen large tents to house themselves on North Windham Road and posted a sign which read, "Strikers Camp of Willimantic. United Textile Workers of America evicted from our homes by the American Thread Company."
Courtesy of Center for Oral History, University of Connecticut

These crumbling brick and stone ruins in Almyville look more like a disaster of war than the neglected remains of a mill or factory. The photograph was taken in 1974, obviously sometime after the building fell into ruins. Incredible as it seems, no one in the area knew what the building had been used for or what had happened to it.
Lee Jacobus photograph; courtesy of the photographer

Only the missing clock hands and the overgrown weeds attest to the desertion of Mansfield Hollow's Kirby Mill in this 1980 photograph. Originally built a hundred years earlier, the granite mill was once home to the National Thread Company, which later sold out to the American Thread Company. While small textile mills couldn't always compete with the giants, other types of mills managed to survive well into the twentieth century by producing unique products. The F. J. Kirby Company, for instance, bought this building in 1907 and converted it into a factory for eyeglass frames (switching to munitions production during World War I). There were many other specialized mills and factories in the area. In Mansfield alone, there was a button mill, a lead pencil factory, and an organ pipe company. Kirby Mill is presently being used as a warehouse by the University of Connecticut.
Courtesy of Center for Oral History, University of Connecticut

The Windham Textile and History Museum opened in 1989 in the former Dunham Hall Building, site of the American Thread Company's offices, library, and company store. The museum has since expanded to include the Dugan Mill next door. Founded as a means of preserving the history of the textile industry, this "living museum" offers changing and permanent exhibits, workshops, and classes.
Courtesy of Windham Textile and History Museum

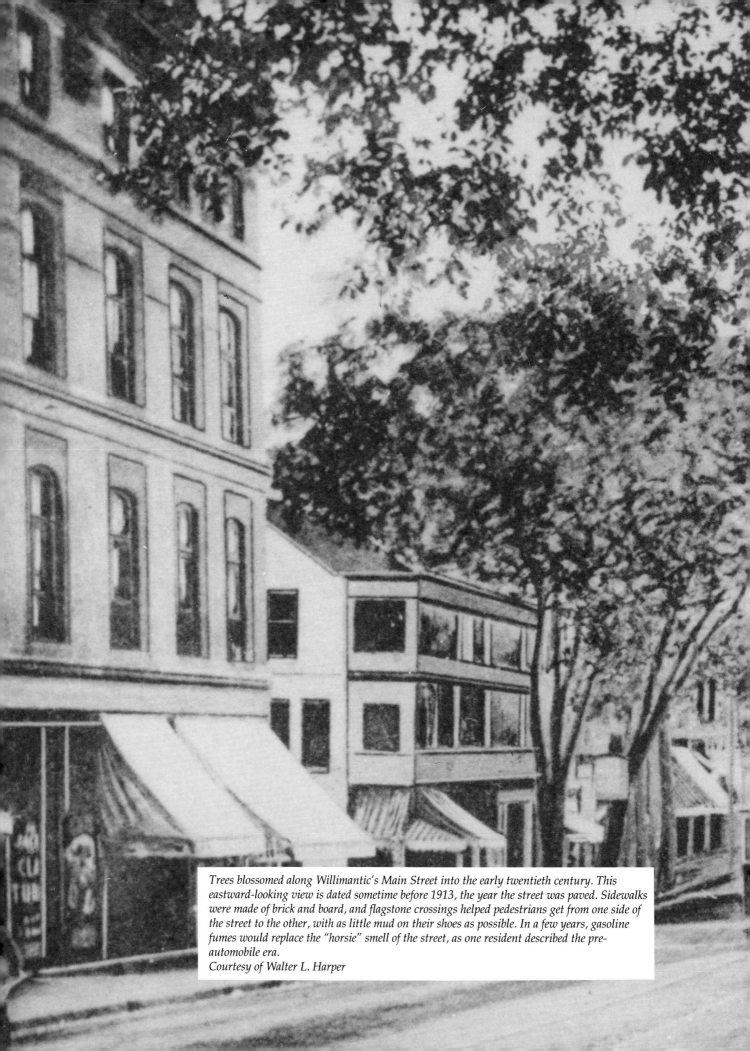

Trees blossomed along Willimantic's Main Street into the early twentieth century. This eastward-looking view is dated sometime before 1913, the year the street was paved. Sidewalks were made of brick and board, and flagstone crossings helped pedestrians get from one side of the street to the other, with as little mud on their shoes as possible. In a few years, gasoline fumes would replace the "horsie" smell of the street, as one resident described the pre-automobile era.
Courtesy of Walter L. Harper

Chapter Three
GATHERING PLACES:
MAIN STREETS AND TOWN GREENS

The origin of America's many Main Streets rests in the New England town. Main Street, itself, stands as a symbol of common national culture and values. "The thickened spine of a New England township" is where it began, but certainly not where American civilization has come.

At first focused upon church, school, or small shop, the region's Main Streets soon became centers of commerce and trade. As homes provided private space, Main Streets offered public space for shoppers, paraders, and those desirous of a stroll. Northeast Connecticut, however, unless in larger communities such as Rockville, Willimantic, and Putnam, still features Main Streets without sidewalks that wind through rural towns and offer little opportunity for such activity. Town greens offer such communities another variety of public space.

They have their origins in the planning of the earliest New England towns, which sought to establish permanent community not simply in the geographic sense, but in a religious and social context as well. For the first among the Puritan settlers, land allocation attempted to bind them into a social unity. Although holding their own land, different families would have to remain in close proximity of one another.

Home lots that could vary from a meager half-acre for a poor bachelor to twenty acres for a wealthy family were set against one or two streets that abutted an area of common land where cattle might be penned and a church built. As time went on and generation succeeded generation, cattle were driven off the commons and the area was refenced and landscaped into the town green.

The green served as the site for churches and other public buildings. Local militias or village guards trained and mustered there. Moreover, one expert observes that early village planners must have realized the advantages and amenities that such open space provided for town dwellers. They recognized the public value of the town green and made openness its major design feature. Another summarized, "Sunniness and space, human scale, natural beauty combined with a garden quality, formality combined with informality—all join hands in the New England green to make it one of the loveliest of American ideas. . . ."

By the end of the nineteenth century, town greens took on functions very different from those envisioned by Puritan planners. In 1875, a baseball diamond was laid out on Columbia's green. Woodstock's

served as a playing ground for th Wabbaquasset Polo Club betweer 1878 and 1888. More than a half century later, in the middle of the twentieth century, the author of a book on village greens of New England would still remark that Connecticut's with their surroun ing buildings "have a charm that sets them apart and they seem to us among the most beautiful" in the region. Her list of "Greens to Enjoy," along with commentary, included the following in the northeast corner:

Bolton Center—Eighteenth- and early nineteenth-century houses cluster around a green where, in the Revolution, Rochambeau's army camped on the march from Newport to the Hudson.

Brooklyn—General Israel Putnam once kept a tavern here and left his plow standing in the field when he went to join the Continental Army.

Coventry—In the minister's house near the green, Nathan Hal prepared for college.

South Woodstock—Elms were planted here to celebrate the Battl of Lexington. They still shade the green.

Vernon Center—The church here. . . . has a square tower with bull's-eye windows and a sharp tapering spire.

Windham—Few greens seem so untouched by today's hustle and bustle as Windham's with its

ell-preserved old buildings
nd fine trees.

Woodstock Hill — A beauti-
lly proportioned Congregational
hurch, an old academy, and a
vern where stagecoaches used to
op are near this peaceful green.

Residents of the region, forty
ears after the making of this list,
ill appeared to appreciate their
wn greens. As gathering places
1 Memorial Day or the Fourth of
ly, they offered welcome public
ace. In 1990, citizens of Hebron
d Tolland advocated the desig-
ation of historical districts in the
ea surrounding their greens,
hich would preserve the integ-
ty and character of abutting
ructures. Tolland's green, a long
d narrow strip, seemed unusual
nong its counterparts, almost a
rassy boulevard with utility
oles running down its quarter-
ile length. To protect the green
self, as one observer commented,
much of the work will be estab-
shing what shouldn't be done to
e land. Simplicity is usually a
irtue in town greens." It might be
uggested that the utility poles
d accompanying wires did not
nhance the area's natural beauty.
n the other hand, modernity
equired such an intrusion on
ature.

Main Street welcomed moder-
ity with its neon lights, hotels,
loons, chain stores, trolley
acks, and automobile congestion.
lere, curbstones marked off the
reet from the sidewalk and signs
enoted the specializations of each
ore, shop, and business. A
hotograph of Willimantic's Main
treet in 1938 (see within) showed
e diversity of the town's central
ommercial area. The eye moves
om the Union Shoe Company to
e A&P supermarket to Mac's
igar Store to Wilson Drug
ompany to Bill's No. 7 Restau-
int to the First National Store to
e Windham Card Shopp and

finally to the old Loomer Opera
House building, which at that time
housed the Bay State Drug Company and Hallock's. Pick up an
old City Directory for your town,
if it was large enough to have one,
and note these cornucopias of
commerce, which the young of
today find in shopping malls far
from Main Street.

Redevelopment wiped out
Rockville's Market Street in 1966.
Previously, it had served as a hub
of business activity and was at the
height of its growth a half century
earlier. Nostalgic for its energy,
residents historically recon-
structed the street:

"At that time next to the drive-
way that led to the railroad tracks
and yard was an electric shop.
Next door Orlando Ransom
operated a grocery store that gave
away green stamps and delivered
orders to the homes in Rockville.
Then came a large wooden block
once owned by the Robertson
family but at that time owned by
George W. Lutz. Here he ran a
hardware store and a carpenter

shop. Under the store the river
rushed and turned a huge over-
shot waterwheel that furnished
power for the machines in the
basement shop. Window frames,
sash, doors, and interior trim for
houses were turned out there.
Over the stores were several
apartments."

They then went on to recount
the Metropolitan Hotel, Herr's
Deli, Heim's Harness Shop, and
Wendheiser Paints. O'Connel's
and Connors' saloons were
separated by the Bishop Fish
Market and conveniently stood
across the street from the railroad
station. It would not be hard for
weary travelers to find a drink.
Further up the street they could
buy ice cream at Gawtrey's or
purchase meat, baked goods or
shoes at other stores; a Chinese
laundry was at their service as
well. Central business streets
obviously offered much to those
who lived in a town or came there
to shop.

They also offered gathering
places for major events. Teddy

*This engraving of Woodstock's green by John Warner Barber
with cows grazing shows one of the earliest uses for a commons. In
the background is the south view of the Congregational Church and
Woodstock Academy is in the central part of the drawing.*

Roosevelt came to speak in Willimantic in August 1902. His train roared to a stop at the junction of Main and Bridge streets, where five thousand people had gathered by 9:00 a.m. At the stop, he and others entered a carriage and rode down the cleared street, which was guarded by a special military detachment from company E. Nine other special carriages followed his to the square at the foot of Church Street; so did the crowd. The brevity of the president's speech did not dilute the political pageantry, which made excellent use of public space. This visit was a special event, but many regularized events put the streets to similar use.

Independence Day, first observed in church ceremony, moved to the street. Initially, early morning parades of "Horribles" would be followed by more serious military displays in the afternoons. Storefronts, lampposts, and buildings were festooned with American flags and colorful bunting for the celebration. Patriotic societies, enthusiastic marching bands, and members of the military paraded. Memorial Day, first set in 1869, originally recognized Civil War veterans; Labor Day celebrated workers as early as 1882. Even earlier, America's Main Streets welcomed the first circus parades. In the 1980s, the city of Willimantic innovated a new form of paradeamania by introducing the "boombox parade." Instead of musical instruments, marchers held all types of radios tuned to a local station, which boomed appropriate music. A new technology came into use for a very traditional purpose. By this time,

Windham Center Green was the scene of the two hundredth anniversary celebration of the founding of the town of Windham held on June 8, 1892. The New England Home Photo Company captured this late afternoon view of the people on the green and the horse-drawn carriages waiting to take them home.
Courtesy of Lucy B. Crosbie and the Willimantic Chronicle

however, other technology had worked to drain Main Street's everyday vitality, although in many larger towns of the region enterprising individuals fought to restore the area's major thoroughfares to their original esteem. Automobiles carried shoppers to outlying malls, which supporters have hailed as America's new town greens and critics have branded the worst symbols of runaway consumerism. Whatever one's point of view, clearly the effect of the shopping mall with its architecture of entertainment in safe enclosed space drew resources away from Main Street. Particularly during the past quarter century, many of these deteriorated, losing stores and businesses and the patrons they

attracted. Run-down streets, boarded-up storefronts, vacant housing scarred the landscape of central business districts. Sometimes, well-meaning attempts at redevelopment decimated areas that were not rebuilt for a long time—or not rebuilt at all. However, the spirit of Main street refused to die as a consequence of efforts to spruce up its facade, recruit new shops and restaurants and offer the amenities provided in its heyday. Despite the modern home's increasing use as an entertainment center based upon television, VCRs, computers, and a variety of electronic games, the public still requires its gathering places. Main Streets and town greens will continue to serve this important purpose.

*...e Scotland Town Green hasn't changed much since this pre-
...orld War I postcard view. The Congregational Church and
...rsonage are still there, along with the post office and general store.
...r over a hundred years, the church had been situated directly on
...e green, but when it burned down in the mid-nineteenth century,
...e new church, shown here, was built across the street.
...urtesy of Walter L. Harper*

*...he gathering on Canterbury's town green offers a classic New England
...ene worthy of Norman Rockwell.
...ourtesy of State Archives, Connecticut State Library*

Coventry's Main Street before it was paved carried many a horse and wagon or carriage and was lined with elegant trees and fine houses with plain and fancy fences.
Courtesy of Frances L. Funk

Trolley tracks on Coventry's Main Street helped move people back and forth to Willimantic until mass transit's demise during the Great Depression. The scene shows the village area with the First Congregational Church in the background.
Courtesy of Walter L. Harper

Willimantic's Footbridge was built in 1906 at a cost of $12,356.83 to "curb the dangerous trespass of children and adults across the railroad yards and walking the tracks over the yard bridge across the Willimantic River to Pleasant Street." The Footbridge is distinctive in that it spans a river, a street, and train tracks. It has been placed on the National Register of Historic Places and is still being used today.
Courtesy of Walter L. Harper

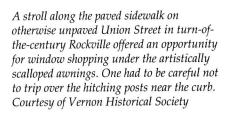

A stroll along the paved sidewalk on otherwise unpaved Union Street in turn-of-the-century Rockville offered an opportunity for window shopping under the artistically scalloped awnings. One had to be careful not to trip over the hitching posts near the curb.
Courtesy of Vernon Historical Society

In the 1880s, Market Street in Rockville was the business hub of Tolland County. Residents from surrounding towns came in by horse and buggy, train, or trolley. The trolley tracks ran down the center of the street with just enough room on either side for a team of horses to pass. The railroad tracks also crossed Market Street, and a flagman was always on duty to halt traffic when necessary. On Saturday nights the street was crowded with shoppers. Besides a variety of retail stores, Market Street had three saloons, a hotel, and an opera house. The street remained a popular shopping area until 1966, when redevelopment obliterated it.
Courtesy of Vernon Historical Society

The City Hotel on South Main Street in Putnam was draped in flags and bunting for the State Firemen's Muster and Parade, September 4, 1900. Store owners and other civic and fraternal organizations spent weeks decorating their storefronts for the parade which featured fire trucks and marchers from all over Connecticut. At the time of the parade, the crowd of onlookers was estimated at ten thousand people. *Courtesy of Aspinock Historical Society of Putnam*

The European House Hotel, on Willimantic's Main Street, was one of five busy hotels in Willimantic. Located in the hotel, the store of D. H. Henken, Merchant Tailor displayed the latest words in gentlemen's clothing. The separate entrance to the hotel's Ladies Dining Saloon on the second floor appears to the right. The European House advertised itself as "headquarters for the traveling man, centrally located, electric lighted, with commodious sample rooms, one block from the railroad station." Salesmen were important clients at hotels as they traveled from town to town with catalogues and cases of their wares. *Courtesy of Lucy B. Crosbie and the Willimantic Chronicle*

Businessmen in Willimantic in 1926 launched a campaign to raise money for a new hotel on Main Street. By creating a friendly competition among themselves to sell shares in the enterprise, they were able to build the Nathan Hale Hotel. They are shown here assembled at the bottom of the Footbridge at Railroad and Main Streets, with a chart marking their fund-raising efforts. One merchant objected to the location of the hotel on Main Street, preferring a suburban location with parking facilities, thus envisioning an early version of a motel. *Courtesy of Greater Willimantic Chamber of Commerce*

The Rotary Club met at the Nathan Hale Hotel on Willimantic's Main Street in the 1950s, some thirty years after the hotel was built with money raised from the businessmen's fund drive. The hotel is now owned by Eastern Connecticut State University. Courtesy of Windham Textile and History Museum

sign charting the progress of the 1910 fund drive to build a YMCA Willimantic was prominently displayed on the Lincoln Furniture tore, a former landmark of Lincoln (now Jillson) Square. The store ood on a triangle of land formed by the junction of Main and Union reets, which was demolished during the 1970s urban renewal roject.
ourtesy of Lucy B. Crosbie and the Willimantic Chronicle

Further west along Willimantic's Main Street stands the Windham Town Hall—still the seat of local government. Its imposing clock tower has told time for the town since 1896, when Mrs. James E. Hayden, wife of the donor of the clock, climbed the tower and started the clock's mechanism. Principal opposition to building the town hall was led by her father-in-law, Whiting Hayden, whose Marble Front building, also on Main Street, housed the Windham town offices and the State Superior Court. When he raised the rent in 1894, the town voted to build its own building. Whiting Hayden died before the new town hall was completed, and his son donated the clock in his memory.
Courtesy of Lucy B. Crosbie and the Willimantic Chronicle

The flag pole dedication on Stafford Springs' Main Street in July 1917 drew a large crowd, partly to hear Rev. Felix O'Neil, the popular poet-priest of St. Edward's Church, and partly to express feelings of patriotism during World War I. The flag pole was donated by Stafford's American Legion chapter, and constructed by local carpenter Washington Graves.
Courtesy of Stafford Historical Society

President Theodore "Teddy" Roosevelt (standing in center foreground) addresses the crowd at Willimantic's Main Street on August 23, 1902. Leaving his special train, Teddy was driven by carriage through long lines of cheering citizens down Main Street, past flag-decked buildings to Lincoln Square, where he spoke for ten minutes. According to the Chronicle, "The city did itself proud as 8,000 people of Willimantic and vicinity cheered the hero of San Juan Hill." Ten days later, in Pittsfield, Massachusetts, on the last day of his New England tour, Roosevelt escaped serious injury when an electric streetcar struck his carriage, gravely injuring his driver, and killing a secret serviceman who was thrown under the trolley.
Courtesy of Lucy B. Crosbie and the
Willimantic Chronicle

Attired in top hats, George Taylor, chairman of Willimantic Old School and Home Week, and Willimantic Mayor Daniel P. Dunn, stand next to portly former President William Howard Taft, center foreground, on the reviewing platform facing Main Street's Town Hall in 1915. The elderly gentlemen to the right may have been in the six-car contingent of Civil War Veterans in the parade that day. Taft, the only man to serve both as president and chief justice of the U.S. Supreme Court, told the crowd assembled at Recreation Park that the parade was "one calculated to show the enterprise and business importance and municipal spirit of Willimantic."
Courtesy of Lucy B. Crosbie and the
Willimantic Chronicle

In spite of World War I raging in Europe, Willimantic's 1915 Old School and Home Week Parade was a festive occasion as the First Regiment's Connecticut National Guard, led by Col. Richard J. Goodman and Captain H. E. Tiesing, approaches what is now Jillson Square. The parade ended at Recreation Park where former President William Howard Taft gave the principal address climaxing the week-long celebration. The Chronicle reported "The weather was perfect and the crowds of people who were here made it the biggest day in the history of the town."
Courtesy of Lucy B. Crosbie and the Willimantic Chronicle

The Willimantic Chronicle described the automobile of merchant H. C. Murray as "decorated all over in white and purple and much admired by everyone who saw it" in the Old School and Home Week Parade of 1915. Mr. Murray sits in the front left, with his driver at the wheel and Mrs. Murray and her guest in the rear seat. Murray's car was followed by two automobiles carrying suffragists with banners that called for "Votes for Women." In 1894, H. C. Murray built a three-story Main Street department store which contained the first automatic elevator in Willimantic.
Courtesy of Lucy B. Crosbie and the Willimantic Chronicle

A float of "Antiques and Horribles," a kind of Halloween-in-July costume party, was a typical feature of many Fourth of July parades down Main Street. In this case, it was one of the highlights of the Vernon-Rockville Centennial in 1908. Other events in the week-long celebration included military and firemen's balls, band concerts, baseball games, balloon ascensions, and an automobile hill-climbing contest.
Courtesy of Vernon Historical Society

This July 4, 1910 parade moves in slightly disorganized array along Willimantic's Main Street, as the float of "horribles" passes by, followed by a contingent of suffragists carrying banners demanding "Votes for Women." The suffragists were booed by some of the men, but cheered by many of the female spectators that day. A parade was more than a routine exercise at the turn of the century; it was a major medium of social expression and loomed large as an exciting event in an otherwise quiet world. Next to Christmas, the Fourth of July was the biggest holiday of the year.
Courtesy of Lucy B. Crosbie and the Willimantic Chronicle

In 1919, Stafford celebrated its Bicentennial with a similar parade down Main Street. Instead of Ancients and Horribles, however, school children from Stafford Springs were dressed in more historic American outfits. Two of them represent Uncle Sam and Miss Liberty, while the others are Indians and Pilgrims. Their attire reflects the increased patriotic mood of the country just after World War I, but what does their spelling of "shool" reflect?
Courtesy of Stafford Historical Society

In 1938, grocery stores like the A&P and the First National in Willimantic were set amidst other Main Street establishments. Large and small businesses abounded, such as the Union Shoe Store, Mac's United Cigars, and Bill's No. 7 Restaurant. The Loomer Opera House down the street would be torn down that year to make room for F. W. Woolsworth's. Trolley tracks recently had been removed.
Courtesy of Lucy B. Crosbie and the Willimantic Chronicle

In spite of the Depression, the newly-built W. T. Grant Company on Willimantic's Main Street had already progressed from a five-and-dime store to a higher priced establishment. Nearly forty years later, Grant's moved to a shopping plaza off Main Street.
Courtesy of Lucy B. Crosbie and the Willimantic Chronicle

In 1974, this Broad Street house was demolished in the $12 million Willimantic Central Business District Urban Renewal Project. Broad Street, which ran parallel to Jackson Street, was eliminated and the land became part of the still vacant major commercial parcel.
Courtesy of Lucy B. Crosbie and the Willimantic Chronicle

By 1970, the home built in 1825 by pioneer Willimantic manufacturer William Jillson, had become an eyesore with broken windows and holes in the roof. Weeds had grown up around the house made of granite blocks quarried from a ledge outcropping on the nearby Willimantic River.
Courtesy of Lucy B. Crosbie and the Willimantic Chronicle

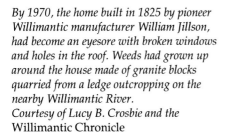

Workers began the restoration of the Jillson House during the Willimantic Urban Renewal Project. The front of the house is on Main Street and the rear door was on that portion of Union Street that would be eliminated during urban renewal.
Courtesy of Lucy B. Crosbie and the Willimantic Chronicle

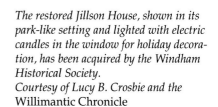

The restored Jillson House, shown in its park-like setting and lighted with electric candles in the window for holiday decoration, has been acquired by the Windham Historical Society.
Courtesy of Lucy B. Crosbie and the Willimantic Chronicle

Barker's Department Store was a Willimantic landmark until replaced by a Super Stop 'n Shop supermarket. The crowded parking lot reflects the movement of shoppers out of the center of town during the post-World War II era to the periphery, where strip development often occurred. Commercial shopping became increasingly decentralized and Main Street could not help but be affected.
Courtesy of Windham Textile and History Museum

The Eastbrook Mall became a further extension of Willimantic area shopping, more distant from the town center than the old Barker's. While small, relative to larger malls west of the region, Eastbrook offered indoor shopping stores to the northeast corner. In this photo, canoers exit the mall probably on their way to outdoors recreational activity.
Bruce M. Stave photograph; courtesy of the photographer

Chapter Four
ON THE ROAD

POST OFFICE

CHARLES POST'S
STORE.

This pre–Civil War photo, dated 1860, is the earliest one in this book, taken only twenty-one years after the invention of photography. Stagecoaches were an important part of rural transportation in Northeast Connecticut well into the nineteenth century, making stops at taverns and post offices along their lines, and carrying news, as well as travelers and mail. This Hebron post office was a regular stop of the Colchester and Andover Mail Stage. Railroads and trolleys gradually led to the demise of the stagecoaches, although at first the stage line companies tried to accommodate themselves to their competitors, by providing transportation to and from train stations.
Courtesy of State Archives, Connecticut State Library

"Without a jar or roll
or antic
Without a stop
at Willimantic
Maids and Matrons, daintily
dimited,
Ride everyday on the
New England
Limited."

While the riders described in this ditty may not have stopped in Willimantic, that town and the others in Northeast Connecticut could not avoid being affected by changes in transportation technology. By foot, horse, carriage, trolley, railroad, automobile, bus, or truck, the people of the region sought means of mobility which ended isolation, connected communities, and expanded horizons of those once limited to a single place. From the beginning of settlement, residents of Tolland and Windham counties were on the road.

Today, like most Americans except for those in the largest cities, they are wedded to private transport and lack effective mass transportation. Traveling in sleekly designed steel boxes or rough hewn pick-up trucks, the inhabitants of Northeast Connecticut's towns pursue privacy in their own automobiles. The individual car permits its owner a freedom of movement throughout the entire region and outside of it as well. This sense of privatism provided by the auto

affects families, too. Many own two or three or even more cars, which allows each family member to go his or her own way; young and old, children and parents cover wide distances for a multitude of purposes. It wasn't always this way.

While today we take for granted the local roads on which we ride, we often forget that they didn't always exist, they weren't always paved, and they lacked direction signs. Their crookedness, even in modern times, often find origin in the paths taken by Indians and early settlers. While our roads are taken for granted, they are also viewed with pride. In 1990, the region's citizens nominated several favorite back roads for scenic road status and placed them within the context of long history or local folklore. The nominator of Old Turnpike in Mansfield claimed it as part of the path taken by Massachusetts Bay colonists, led by Rev. Thomas Hooker, who went west to establish a settlement in Hartford during the fourth decade of the seventeenth century; he also suggested George Washington traveled it in 1789 enroute from Boston to the then nation's capital of New York. A partisan of Codfish Falls Road noted it followed a path laid out in the eighteenth century to connect Gurleyville Village to the Boston-Hartford Turnpike, now Route 44. Whatever

the community, roads played an important role in their history and development.

More than a hundred years before the founding of Willington, Mohegan Indians built a trail which became the town's first road; by 1886, Willington had built a hundred miles of highway. However, seven years later a new doctor decided not to practice there because he found the roads in such poor condition. One historian of that community's development observed the importance of road building to townspeople by analyzing the percentage of items relating to roads that dominated town meetings. From the beginning of the nineteenth century through 1900, when education became the most discussed item, road construction and repairs occupied the bulk of town meeting agendas.

Early settlers trod the roads by foot, horse, and carriage. Stage routes developed and in 1783 Somers was linked to Hartford and then Hartford to Boston and Boston to New York, the full trip taking four days and costing $10. Transportation helped build a network of cities and towns. With the advent of the railroad the velocity of network building intensified. However, the practicality of the railroad did not seem a given to early nineteenth century observers. Perhaps the story is apocryphal, but when a school

74

The horse and buggy—or the horse and sled in winter—were the main means of private transportation in the late nineteenth and early twentieth centuries before the invention or widespread use of the automobile. These examples are both from Putnam, but such scenes were common throughout Northeast Connecticut.
Courtesy of Aspinock Historical Society of Putnam

it allegedly responded, "You are welcome to use the schoolhouse to debate all proper questions, but such things as railroads are impossibilities and rank infidelity. God never designed that His intelligent creatures should travel at the frightful speed of fifteen miles an hour." His creatures chose to do otherwise—and at much greater speeds.

Despite opposition from landowners concerned that their fields would be overrun and stagecoach, canal, and turnpike companies which feared competition, the state and the region found itself at the center of a web of rails. By the late 1830s, five mile of track connected Rhode Island and Stonington, which then linked by steamer to New York City; in 1838, Hartford and New Haven were connected and six years later, New Haven tied into New York City by rail. By 1855, Connecticut had six hundred miles of track and Northeast Connecticut was part of the network. The Norwich and Worcester Railroad opened in 1840 and would move south to the docks in New London and north to Worcester through depots which included Danielson, Dayville, Putnam, and North Grosvenordale. "Southerners" from New London stimulated additional railroad growth in the northeastern section when they incorporated the New London, Willimantic and Springfield Railroad in May 1847. Facing a depression in the whaling industry and recognizing the importance of rail connections, the New London city fathers maintained that a rail line was essential; otherwise, "the city is done forever . . . her fate is sealed."

Such anxiety drove railroadmania, as did its reverse — a boundless faith in the potential of the new technology. In Willimantic, businessmen such as William Jillson promoted their stop on the line believing that if the railroad bypassed them, the city "would fail in becoming one of the largest and most important inland towns in the country." Other towns joined the railroad bandwagon and the company incorporated in 1847 merged a

76

ear later into the New London,
illimantic, and Palmer, the
assachusetts town which re-
aced Springfield as northern-
ost terminus.

Stafford Springs welcomed the
pportunity by encouraging the
ne to pass right through the
nter of town and by its residents
uying stock in amounts second
ly to the New Londoners;
sidents of the Merrow section of
ansfield contributed cash for a

sidetrack to unload materials near
them. Hence, the basis of the later
Central Vermont was established.
It would climb from the south in
New London through areas such
as Lebanon, South Windham,
Willimantic, South Coventry,
Eagleville, Mansfield Depot,
Merrow, the South and West
Willingtons, and Stafford Springs.
The Willimantic promoters prob-
ably felt vindicated when, by the
end of the nineteenth century,

their city became one of the hubs
of New England railroading with
nearly forty trains a day passing
through; it served as an important
interchange for the New Haven
and New England railroads.

Early in the twentieth century,
the Central Vermont began
passenger service from New
London to Montreal, but by mid-
century passenger railroading in
the United States generally declined and the region was no

exception. Cars substituted for passenger trains; and trucks replaced freights as major means of conveyance for goods. While the demise of railroading reflected the victory of private transit over mass transportation, Northeast Connecticut residents tried at least one other form of mass transit that other Americans found popular in the late nineteenth century and early decades of the twentieth. In large cities throughout the nation, first horse railways, then electric street railroads or trolleys served to shorten distances between periphery and center and to allow for increased distance between places of work and residence. Developers often promoted trolley lines so that new areas for construction could be opened. The trolley played an important role in shaping urban America.

It played an equally important role for a number of decades in rural Northeast Connecticut linking neighborhoods within towns and towns to others within the region. For instance, the year 1893 witnessed the incorporation of the Hartford, Manchester and Rockville Tramway Company, the Putnam and Thompson Street Railroad Company, and the People's Tramway Company, which bought out the Putnam and Thompson in 1899; by 1902, it had been merged into the Consolidated Railway Company. The Willimantic Traction Company formed in 1901 and sold out to Consolidated in 1905. By 1910, Connecticut had about one thousand miles of trolley lines and citizens greeted the coming of the electric street railways with great expectation. They offered speedy

and clean transport, doing away with the messy horse droppings that had polluted town streets for such a long time.

For some, the trolleys offered new opportunities for fun and leisure activity. A Willimantic woman remembered that everyone hopped on the trolley to Coventry on Saturday nights to go to dances. "The boys used to jump on the sides and sway it about. The old man who drove the trolley cursed them, and the young girls screamed. You thought they were going to tip it over. It was our idea of a good time. . . ."

In Stafford, when the Hartford to Stafford via Rockville run began on April 20, 1908, the town was festooned with red, white, and blue bunting. Expectant crowds joined with prominent officials to celebrate the occasion, which was topped off with a fireworks display. Thirteen miles separated Stafford and Rockville, which the street railway made in forty minutes; it took another hour to reach the state capital. Each segment of the trip could be done for a quarter's fare compared to the $2.00 and five hours it took to travel the same distance by stage. However, what seemed a boon in 1908 made its last run in 1928. Many other companies shut down during the Great Depression. The economy and the competition from automobiles and buses put them out of business. Afterwards, mass transit never regained its ascendancy in moving people, although some successes, limited at best, can be counted. For example, in 1906 promoters planned a trolley line from Willimantic to Stafford Springs by way of Storrs.

It never was built. Not until three quarters of a century later in 1980 did the first public transportation between Storrs and Willimantic get established.

The lure of the auto with its promise of privacy, personal freedom to move when and where one wished, and general convenience overcame the seemingly less convenient mass transport. America and Northeast Connecticut fell in love with the horseless carriage. In the United States, the 8,000 motor vehicles of 1900 grew to 485,000 by 1910 and within another half decade the number reached 2.5 million. After World War I automobile ownership increased greatly. By 1919, there was one auto for every sixteen Americans and the market seemed to be saturated. By 1928, the ratio stood at one to six and, as one observer noted, with a little crowding the entire population of the nation could have been on the highway at the same time; Americans registered 23,122,000 autos and 4,380,000 trucks.

A Putnam resident, early in the century, described his first ride, "Ten to twelve miles per hour was about the best speed. It produced no strain on the machinery nor any disturbing jar of the nerves, as would a swifter speed." A local newspaper reported that in Willington in 1902, "An automobile appeared recently on the hill. It came from the south but exactly whence it came and whither it went nobody seemed to know." During Christmas, 1911, M. R. Joy, the first auto salesman in Putnam, who operated, as was common for early auto people, a local livery stable, advertised a Pope-Hartford

...ouring car for $3,000. With the ...dvent of Henry Ford's mass ...roduced Model T, residents of ...at city could purchase an auto ...r considerably less. By the time ...World War I, Dodge Brothers ...otor Car offered a car or road-...er for $785; winterized it would ...ost $950. The region almost ...ecame a center of automobile ...roduction, but the Hebron-...ased Amston Motor Car Com-...any failed in 1917. Nevertheless, ...e auto had left its mark. A ...gn of the times came in ...illington in 1927 when the old

horse sheds behind the Congregational Church were torn down. Automobiles,not horses, brought people to worship.

It seemed, however, that people often worshipped their automobiles. While the Depression may have made them too expensive for the average citizen and World War II created a scarcity of gasoline and rationing, post–World War II America, including Northeast Connecticut, intensified its love affair with the car. The federal government promoted this long before. The Federal Roads

Act of 1916 and the Federal Highway Act of 1921 helped ease America's pace on the road; the Interstate Highway Act of 1956 linked region to region, state to state, and made areas such as Northeast Connecticut more accessible to the outside world. Familiar with Interstates 84, 95, 384, 395, and 91, as well as state and local highways, the residents of the quiet corner for quite some time have been on the road.

These photographs seem to come from different eras, but both were taken in 1918. During the spring muddy season, horse and wagon was the only means of travel along North Eagleville Road, the route that linked Storrs with the train station in Eagleville, three miles away. The "stage line" from the Connecticut Agricultural College met three trains daily. The Studebaker jitney, or "autobus," ran between Storrs and Willimantic on Route 195, a more highly traveled road maintained by the state, although not paved until 1930. The driver of the jitney also provided a shopping service, accepting small commissions at ten cents an item.
Courtesy of Historical Manuscripts and Archives, University of Connecticut Library

The town of Columbia provided a horse-drawn sled or wagon (depending on the weather) to transport students to Windham High School in 1915. Until then, transportation was the financial responsibility of each family, which meant that many students didn't continue their education past the eighth grade. Those who could afford it took the train to Willimantic and then walked a mile to the high school. Riding in the sled had its disadvantages, however. Students often got so cold they would get out and run alongside the sled to keep warm.
Courtesy of Columbia Historical Society

The first motorized school bus to bring out-of-town students to Windham High School was from Willington in 1923. Before then, Willington students, like those from surrounding towns, had to take the train to Willimantic in order to attend high school. Bus driver Art Devereaux, not shown, was a much-loved driver in those early days. In 1990, Willington discontinued sending students to Windham High School, switching to E. O. Smith in Mansfield.
Courtesy of Walter L. Harper

One of the earliest examples of the horseless carriage is shown in this 1901 photograph taken in front of the Grosvenor Dale Company Fire Department. The fire department stood next to the Grosvenor Dale Company mill, which built and operated the fire station for its own use. The building is draped in mourning after the assassination of President McKinley.
Courtesy of Thompson Historical Society

With the advent of cars, the surface of the roads changed from dirt to cement. The first cement road in Connecticut was Route 12 in the North Grosvenordale section of Thompson. Tony Vito is shown guiding his steamroller in this circa 1914 photograph of the construction process, taken by Plainfield photographer John Prior. Courtesy of Thompson Historical Society

The present-day Route 44 began as an eighteenth-century highway, cutting through many towns in Northeast Connecticut as it connected Boston and Hartford. George Washington travelled this old toll road on his 1789 inaugural tour, passing through the Mansfield Four Corners, shown here in this late nineteenth-century postcard, on his way to breakfast at the Brigham Tavern in Coventry. Inns and public houses were welcome sights for weary travelers along the length of the Hartford Turnpike, also known as the Boston Turnpike and Middle Turnpike, depending on one's destination. Fuller's Tavern (left) was a Mansfield landmark at the intersection until it was torn down in the 1930s. Notice that the road to the right (now Route 195) doesn't continue north past the intersection.
Courtesy of Walter L. Harper

Mansfield's Four Corners has changed from a sleepy country crossing to a highly travelled intersection, with the continuation of Route 195 north into Tolland, and a plethora of gas stations, banks, and restaurants on every side. Yet the basic contour of Route 44 remained the same for many years.
Bruce M. Stave photograph; courtesy of the photographer

The horseless carriage was still considered a luxury in 1910 when Ernest P. Chesbro, who had been a dealer in wagons and carriages, opened an auto store in Willimantic, where he sold Buicks and Overlands. The latter cost between $1,000 and $1,500, with glass front screen and gas tank extra. Pictured from left to right are Fred Little, E. P. Chesbro, Leslie Nichols, Walter Brown, and John Upton. Courtesy of Lucy B. Crosbie and the Willimantic Chronicle

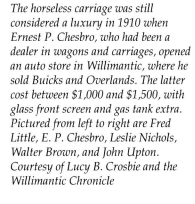

A decade later, the automobile was becoming commonplace, but in this circa 1920 photograph of the Franklin Automobile Agency in Putnam, one can still see signs of other modes of transportation — the livery stable next door and the trolley tracks in front of the cars. This dealership proudly displays a Harley motorcycle and three Franklin cars in its streetside show-room. Courtesy of Aspinock Historical Society of Putnam

Mr. and Mrs. Fred Brunell stand in front of their combination gas station and ice cream sta[n]
in Somers, in 1926. This early roadside establishment appealed to the growing number of
automobile owners out for a Sunday drive. The building still stands along route 190 and is
used by children for a playhouse.
Courtesy of Somers Historical Society

Aldrich estate in Pomfret.
Courtesy of Quinebaug Valley Community College Library

Most early automobiles were open run-abouts and touring cars, with convertible tops and flimsy side curtains for inclement weather. Probably the most popular car was the Model T Ford, which became affordable during World War I because its assembly-line production rapidly lowered the price. In 1917, it cost $360. The photo of the woman by the side of the road shows a somewhat earlier version of the Model T, circa 1912-1914. The 1915 Dodge Brothers roadster was perfect for this Putnam family's Sunday outing, and the Packard touring car, circa 1918, was luxurious enough to boast a chauffeur and footman in front of the Aldrich estate in Pomfret.

Many trolley companies had names like "The People's Tramway Company," in Danielson, which emphasized their accessibility to a broad public. However, when trolleys first came into use during the nineteenth century, fares often were too high for the average worker. Before the turn of the century, many political reformers included the "five cents fare" on a plank in their platforms.
Courtesy of Aspinock Historical Society of Putnam

In 1899, the People's Tramway Company began operating open-air summer trolleys between Putnam and Alexander's Lake, a four-mile trip that took forty-five minutes each way. By the following year, the company had developed the area around the lake into a fashionable resort called Wildwood Park, featuring a lake pavilion, a dancing pavilion, and a two-story building for parties. Saturday night dances were a popular entertainment at Wildwood Park, although many people visited just for the trolley ride. The photo, circa 1905, was taken at the corner of Elm and Front streets in Putnam.
Courtesy of Aspinock Historical Society of Putnam

The all-male passengers in this early chartered bus in Ballouville, a section of Killingly, are on their way to Rocky Point, Rhode Island, for a shore dinner. By not being limited to tracks, buses offered the opportunity for direct travel.
Courtesy of Quinebaug Valley Community College Library

All aboard for Baltic in 1910. When the Willimantic Traction Company laid trolley tracks from Norwich to Willimantic, and stopped in Taftville, Baltic, and Franklin, passengers gained a mode of public transportation that was convenient and pleasant, and the motorman would stop the car so you could retrieve your hat if it blew off. Courtesy of Lucy B. Crosbie and the Willimantic Chronicle

SCHEDULE OF OPERATIONS OF CERTIFICATE NO. 30
EASTERN STANDARD TIME
HARTFORD AND WILLIMANTIC JITNEY ASSOCIATION, INC.

HARTFORD TO WILLIMANTIC
DAILY

Miles	Fare	Leave	1 A.M.	2 A.M.	3 A.M.	4 A.M.	5 M.	6 P.M.	7 P.M.	8 P.M.	9 P.M.	10 P.M.	11 P.M.	12 P.M.
0	$0.00	Hartford		7:30	9:00	10:30	12:00	1:15	3:00	4:15	6:00	8:00		10:00
8.5	.75	Manchester		7:55	9:25	10:55	12:25	1:40	3:25	4:40	6:25	8:25		10:25
13.0	.75	Bolton Notch		8:05	9:35	11:05	12:35	1:50	3:35	4:50	6:35	8:35		10:35
19.0	1.00	Andover		8:20	9:50	11:20	12:50	2:05	3:50	5:05	6:50	8:50		10:50
28.1	1.25	Willimantic		8:45	10:15	11:45	1:15	2:30	4:15	5:30	7:15	9:15		11:15
	2.25	Danielson		10:00			1:10	2:30		5:30	6:40			
	3.25	Providence, Ar.		11:15			2:45	3:30			7:55	8:15		

Sp. Sun. and Holidays

WILLIMANTIC TO HARTFORD
DAILY

Miles	Fare	Leave	A.M.	A.M.	A.M.	A.M.	M.	P.M.	P.M.	P.M.	P.M.	P.M.	P.M.	P.M.
0	$0.00	Willimantic	6:15	7:30	9:00	10:30	12:00	1:30	3:00	4:30	6:00	7:00	8:00	10:00
9.1	50	Andover	6:40	7:55	9:25	10:55	12:25	1:55	3:25	4:55	6:25	7:25	8:25	10:25
14.5	.75	Bolton Notch	6:50	8:10	9:40	11:10	12:40	2:10	3:40	5:10	6:40	7:40	8:40	10:40
18.9	1.00	Manchester	7:05	8:20	9:50	11:20	12:50	2:20	3:50	5:20	6:50	7:50	8:50	10:50
28.1	1.25	Hartford	7:30	8:45	10:15	11:45	1:15	2:45	4:15	5:45	7:15	8:15	9:15	11:15

Special Sun. and Holidays

IMPORTANT—READ THE FOLLOWING

Trip No. 1 does not run Sundays or holidays.
Trips 2-4-6-8 connect for Danielson, Providence, Putnam and Woonsocket.
Trips 1-2-8-12 connect for North and South Coventry. Trip No. 5 connects Saturday only.
Trips 2-4-6 connect for Stafford Springs. Trips 2-6-8 connect for Storrs.
Trips 3-5-7 connect for Columbia, Hebron and Colchester. Trip No. 9 connects for Danielson.
All trips connect at Willimantic with buses and trolleys for Norwich and New London.
Connections at Hartford with buses for Winsted, Torrington, New Haven, Waterbury and Springfield.
In effect April 25, 1926.   **REDUCED THROUGH FARE TO PROVIDENCE—3.25**   (over)

The Hartford and Willimantic Jitney Association had a fleet of large automobiles similar to today's limousines, that ran on a regular schedule between various cities and towns. In 1926, there were nine round trips daily for the 28.1 mile journey which took one hour and fifteen minutes and cost $1.25. You could leave Willimantic in the morning, shop and see a picture show in Hartford, and be home in time for supper. A network of jitney routes provided direct connections for Columbia, Hebron, and Colchester; Pomfret, Danielson, and Providence; Coventry and Stafford Springs. All trips connected at Willimantic with buses and trolleys for Norwich and New London. Courtesy of Lucy B. Crosbie and the Willimantic Chronicle

The trolley era only lasted about thirty-five years, but at its zenith it provided fierce competition to the railroads. Starting in 1904, the New Haven Railroad began to buy up all the Connecticut trolley lines as if they were going out of style, which indeed they were, on the eve of Henry Ford's assembly-line production of automobiles. Most of the trolley lines ended in financial ruin, and the interest on the 120 million dollar acquisition program was a drain on the New Haven Railroad for the next fifty years. The New Haven organized the New England Transportation Company, whose buses replaced the trolley, and successfully petitioned the Public Utilities commission to abandon the trolley line in Willimantic on this day in 1936.
Courtesy of Lucy B. Crosbie and the **Willimantic Chronicle**

The South Coventry station was one of the stops on the Central Vermont Railway line, along with Stafford Springs, West Willington, South Willington, Merrow, Mansfield Depot, Eagleville, Willimantic, and South Windham. Several of those depots have disappeared, but the South Coventry station is still standing. Livery service, the forerunner of the taxicab, was available at many stations. It could be had "with or without drivers," according to an advertisement of the day. The signs on the station wall post the mileage to Brattleboro, the northernmost stop, at 86.2 miles, and to New London, the southernmost, at 34.8 miles.
Courtesy of Walter L. Harper

These Hampton passengers wait patiently for the train to arrive, perhaps the fabled New England Limited that ran between Willimantic and Boston, making stops in East Thompson, Putnam, and Pomfret as well as Hampton. It was in Hampton that the luxurious train, nicknamed "The White Train" for its white and gold exterior, became snowbound during the Blizzard of 1888, unable to climb the steep grade outside the Hampton station. Luckily the dining car, seven parlor cars, and four passenger coaches provided food and a place to sleep for the stranded passengers. The milk train also stopped in Hampton on its way to Boston, and farmers from Chaplin, Ashford, and Eastford, as well as Hampton, filled up a railway car with milk cans every morning. Courtesy of Walter L. Harper

The Central Vermont Railway came to Stafford in 1850 connecting it south to Willimantic and New London, and north to Vermont, as well as points west. At a time when the town was losing popularity as a resort, the railroad brought in new business, with both passenger and freight trains. Today, the freight train still passes through town once or twice a day, but no longer stops at the red brick station, which is shared by the Stafford Historical Society and the Golden Agers, a senior citizens' organization. Courtesy of Walter L. Harper

Putnam was once one of the busiest railroad junctions in Northeast Connecticut, ranking just behind Willimantic with thirty trains a day passing through. The train on the left was arriving from Boston on its way to New York. The train on the right was coming from Worcester going south to New London. Besides passenger trains making frequent arrivals and departures, freight cars filled the railroad yard, bringing in raw materials for the mills and taking away finished goods. The Chickering House (left center) was a hotel frequented by salesmen trying to solicit business in the mills. The photograph, circa 1890, shows the old Union Station, since replaced and now commercially occupied. Courtesy of Aspinock Historical Society of Putnam

The men of the Willimantic railroad station pose in front of the engine of a New York, New Haven, and Hartford train in 1908. That rail line was one of many that passed through the city, making Willimantic one of the most convenient and accessible railroad centers in the country. The depot was built at the foot of Railroad Street, the hub of a business district that included stores, restaurants, newsstands, and saloons. Courtesy of Windham Textile and History Museum

Willimantic photographer Julian Beville took this circa 1900 picture of a train crew posing on the tracks in front of a train. Courtesy of Lucy B. Crosbie and the Willimantic Chronicle

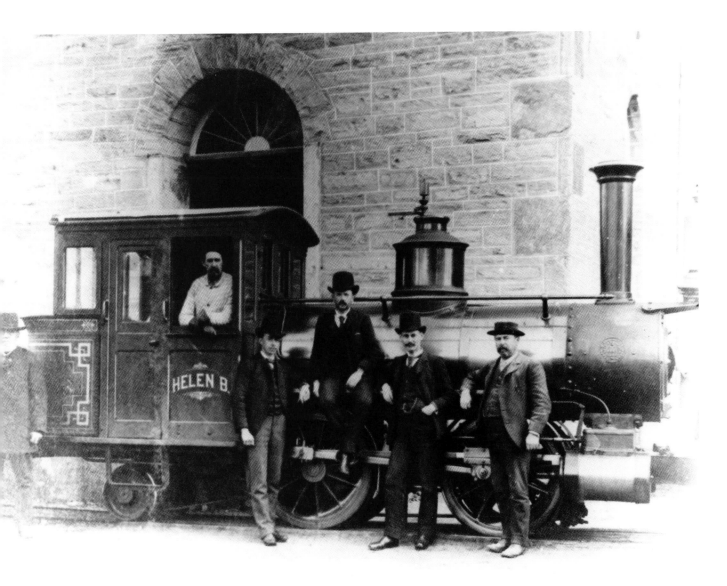

The engine of the Willimantic Linen Company steam railroad train
was named for Helen Boss, daughter of General Eugene Boss, the
agent in charge of the mill in 1893, when this photograph was taken.
The train shuttled back and forth from the railroad siding unloading
freight cars filled with the long fiber Egyptian cotton that came first
by boat to New London, and the shorter fiber Southern cotton that
came north by train. The narrow-gauge train traveled from the main
mill complex across the company's private bridge over the
Willimantic River to the spectacular Mill No. 4.
Courtesy of Lucy B. Crosbie and the Willimantic Chronicle

The railroad brought the Liberty Bell through many towns in Northeast Connecticut in 1903, on its way to Boston for the 128 anniversary of the Battle of Bunker Hill. The stop here is in Plainfield, a historic moment for baby Helen Ashley, her mother Alice, standing near her, and her grandfather Edward Ashley, the man with the beard.
Courtesy of Aspinock Historical Society of Putnam

The Budd Car was a last-ditch effort by the New York, New Haven, and Hartford Railroad to revive a dying passenger train service, which had become completely overshadowed by the automobile. These self-propelled, diesel cars, manufactured by the Budd Company, had been used in the thirties and reinstated in the fifties. Three years after this 1952 photograph, however, the flood of 1955 washed out the railroad bridge in Putnam, and the New York, New Haven, and Hartford Railroad decided it wasn't worth the expense of rebuilding it, thus ending the era of passenger trains in Northeast Connecticut, until the revival of the Montrealer in 1991. Pictured, left to right, are J. Francis Moriarty, Windham town clerk; "Buck" Dumaine, Jr., president of the New Haven Railroad; Christine Meyer, Willimantic Chamber of Commerce secretary; James F. Malone, Chronicle editor; E. J. McCabe, Chamber of Commerce executive director; William Sledjeski, Chamber president; and an unidentified railroad representative.
Courtesy of Greater Willimantic Chamber of Commerce

This abandoned bus in North Grosvenordale is a reminder—and perhaps an ominous symbol—of our changing modes of transportation. Having foregone mass transit in favor of the private automobile, we may yet have to revive older systems of transport, as well as develop new ones, in order to save our economy and ecology.
Lee Jacobus photograph; courtesy of the photographer.

Chapter Five
SCHOOLS & SOCIETY

Fifty years after Miss Abbott's primary class at Natchaug School posed in 1888, Ernest C. Whitaker of Boston sent this picture to the Willimantic Chronicle and identified himself by the arrow at left ("E"). Of his classmates he could only identify his friend Johnny Robinson ("J") and a girl in the middle of the picture he remembered as Winnie ("W"). This wooden Natchaug School built in 1864 was torn down in 1914 to make way for the brick building now on the site. Courtesy of Lucy B. Crosbie and the Willimantic Chronicle

Education is the product of many factors in American society. Family, friends, church, and mass culture all educate, even if informally. Schools are the formal institutions to which society assigns the task of educating. Sometimes this is done successfully; at other times it is not. In America, education is frequently aligned with the ideas of democracy and equality despite the fact that education may reinforce inequality as one receives knowledge and credentials that others do not have. Schooling reflects and reinforces society's values and to this Connecticut and the northeastern region was no exception. Primary, secondary, and higher education left an indelible mark on the northeast corner of the state.

Connecticut's first school law, embraced in the Code of 1650, decreed that all towns with fifty families should employ a teacher to instruct children to read and write. Hence, from the outset of the colony, religious and economic motives prompted Connecticut to encourage education. From that time to the end of the eighteenth century, control and financing of education increasingly became the responsibility of towns. Initially, church societies played a strong role in determining school policy such as the location of schools, the length of a term, the choice of teachers, and the cost to each

student and the society generally.

Rotation of school location was not uncommon. For instance, the Pomfret First Society chose to hold school "eight weeks at the north, seven at the west, seven at the south, and four at Wappaquasett." The amount of time assigned to an area frequently depended on its wealth as evidenced by the grand list. Students had the opportunity to follow schools from location to location, but usually attended only when it met in their area. By the middle of the eighteenth century, most church societies ended such rotation and established permanent schools in each district. In 1795, legislation terminated church control over education and placed it in the hands of school committees or selectmen, who tended to economize when making educational policy. The General Assembly's Common School Fund based upon interest from the sale of land in the Western Reserve didn't help matters. As in modern times, some townspeople felt the fund diluted local control; others maintained local decisions gave too much consideration to how much money cold be obtained from the fund rather than on real needs.

In Tolland, the first school societies were formed in 1798 so that eventually thirteen school districts existed, each with a one-room schoolhouse; districts developed wherever fifty or more

families lived. By 1800, Stafford witnessed eleven districts overseen by its First Society and seven by its Second. Willington's school passed from religious to School Society hands in 1798, but church influence didn't disappear; clergy and divinity students, earning money for college, served as teachers. Schoolrooms provided sites for Sunday catechism and religious meetings. Moreover, families often boarded teachers as part of their compensation.

Not only were teachers and students brought into such close proximity at home, but one-room schoolhouses brought pupil of all ages together. Students often shared desks and the pre-blackboard slates on which they wrote their lessons. Only later did paper, pencils, pens and inkwells come; often parents had to pay individually for supplies. Teacher stressed the "Three Rs" and sometimes did not spare the rod for disciplinary problems. The words "School days, school days, Dear old Golden Rule Days; Reading and 'Riting and 'Rithmetic; Taught to the tune of a Hickory Stick" did not appear without meaning.

Not only did teachers instruct the youth of the entire community but they tended wood-burning potbellied stoves and cleaned the premises as well, often with the help of an older, usually male, student. Smoke from these stoves d poor lighting sometimes ade their and their charges' sks difficult. If a winter's storm ft its trail, the teacher frequently d the responsibility of having e path to the road shoveled. The ne-room schoolhouse reflected e lack of specialization of an rlier era in our history. In rural ortheast Connecticut, they lasted ell into the twentieth century; for stance, Stafford's continued ntil 1940, Union's until 1950, and shford's until 1952.

Education, of course, grew far ore complex, giving rise to rger, more bureaucratic (and odern) institutions. Already by 868, Connecticut's public pri-

mary schools were supported by taxes and/or state aid and termed "free"; high schools joined this category in 1872. The state, however, also witnessed the growth of academies or private schools, which prepared students beyond common school training. Young men might train for college; young women, who were much less likely to go on to college, as was the prejudice of the day, prepared for "their social responsibilities." Several of the earliest academies for men opened in the state's northeast corner with Woodstock Academy dating from 1801 and Bacon Academy from 1803; Pomfret

began at the end of the century in 1894. Perhaps the academy which made the most historically significant mark did so not because of its educational impact and longevity but because of its brevity of existence and what it tells us about the racism of its day.

In 1831, a Quaker schoolmistress, Prudence Crandall, began a school in Canterbury for young ladies of some of the area's "best families." When she determined to admit a black student, who wouldn't even have boarded at the school but would have lived with her father elsewhere, whites boycotted. Then, with assistance from Abolitionists such as William

ne-room schoolhouses, like the Somers school shown here, were scattered around each town accommodate children in outlying rural areas in the days before school buses. Somers had one-room schools; other towns had up to a dozen. Gradually these district schools were nsolidated into a more centralized system, but a few one-room schoolhouses remained in use towns like Ashford until the 1950s. Many of the old schoolhouses have been converted to her uses, including private residences, retail stores, and even a fire station. urtesy of Somers Historical Society

Lloyd Garrison and Lewis Tappan, schoolmistress Crandall decided to open a school exclusively for "young ladies and little misses of color." That didn't sit well with the locals, who insulted her, broke windows and engaged in other vandalism, and had her arrested for violating a state law that forbade the teaching of Negroes who were not state residents. The school closed in 1834, but the building in which it was located exists today as a museum—and a reminder of the incident. At the end of the twentieth century, as the nation's educational institutions continued to grapple with the issue of racism, a small building in Northeast Connecticut offers a lesson to us all, and not a happy one at that.

The relationship of schools to race and ethnicity, then, is nothing new. Schools have been seen as vehicles for social mobility and assimilation. One patronizing observer of Willimantic's Irish in 1885, while deprecating the Irish immigrant mill workers, noted that as a result of common schooling, the immigrants' children

improved over their parents, the next generation even more so, and the next "could scarcely be distinguished from Americans." For adults already too old for such schooling, some communities established night schools for the foreign born as Columbia did in 1927 (see photograph within). This particular attempt at educating and "Americanizing" lasted until 1933 and represented one response to the perceived needs of the newcomers and of the society into which they came. Obviously, contemporary issues such as bilingualism have a long history and are not new to our time.

Nor is the importance of higher education to the northeast corner. With the founding of Yale College in 1701, Connecticut, after Massachusetts and Virginia, took the lead in establishing an institution of higher learning. While it would take another 180 years for Tolland County to become a seat of higher

learning, and initially a modest one at that, the provision of advanced learning has become central to the area. When the University of Connecticut was first established in 1881 as the Storrs Agricultural School, it inherited Yale's land-grant status and symbolized a popular reaction to that institution's program of classical education and elitism. Farm organizations such as the Grange pointed out that the New Haven college's entrance requirements "virtually barred farm boys."

The new agricultural school began on 170 acres of land and with a gift of $5,000 from the brothers Augustus and Charles Storrs, who were natives of Mansfield, but at the time of their gifts lived in Brooklyn, Connecticut. It admitted women a dozen years after its founding and became the Connecticut Agricultural College in 1899, the Con-

One of the biggest expenses to running a one-room schoolhouse was the wood for the potbelly stove, like this one in North Ashford (part of the town of Eastford). The teacher's salary was small in comparison. In fact, young women made up to seven times as much in the mills as they did in teaching, particularly in rural communities.
Courtesy of Ruth Smith

cticut State College in 1933, and
e University of Connecticut in
39. While in the beginning Yale
ucated ministers, doctors and
wyers, UConn, as it came to be
own, began by educating the
ns and daughters of farmers and
echanics. Today, it is a
ultiveristy with 26,250 students,
,000 alumni, and a 3,100 acre
mpus at Storrs and other cam-
ses around the state. As a leader
research, teaching, and public
rvice, it ranks among the
tion's top state universities.

However, it is not alone in
oviding higher education in the
gion. Eight years after its found-
g, the state legislature selected
illimantic in 1889 as one of the
es for a normal school to pro-
de teacher training. Tuition was
ee, provided students promised
teach in Connecticut; room and
ard was $3.50 per week. In 1937,
e two-year Willimantic Normal
hool became the four-year

Willimantic State Teachers College, which in 1959 dropped
teachers from its name and eight
years later became Eastern Connecticut State College; in 1983, it
was renamed Eastern Connecticut
State University and stood as part
of a large state university system,
which incorporated four regional
schools. Each name change reflected a broadening of the
school's educational mission until
today when it serves a student
body of approximately 4,500.
Finally, with the establishment of
Quinebaug Valley Community
College in 1971, the multipurpose
nature of higher education in the
region broadened even further.

The breadth of education had
already widened for the region
and the state when in 1917, the
Connecticut Training School for
the Feeble-Minded (formerly the
Connecticut School for Imbeciles)
and the Connecticut Colony for
Epileptics were combined into the

Mansfield Training School and
Hospital. The School went on to
become a model for training of
the retarded, but it also suffered
from the problems faced by such
institutions, especially when
budgets were restricted. In recent
times, the movement toward
deinstitutionalization and its
emphasis on small group living
has reduced the MTS to a shadow
of its once renowned reputation.

Hence, education in Tolland
and Windham counties played an
important role in shaping the
region's culture and society.
Formalized institutions such as
public and private schools,
colleges and universities, libraries
and museums pass on knowledge
and learning from one generation
to another. Nevertheless, we must
remember that cultural values are
transferred in other ways as
well—family, friends, church, and
the media all serve to educate.
Through formal and informal
means, the people of the northeast
corner have learned, learn, and
will learn. This is a lesson worth
remembering.

*Joseph Kratochvil was the only eighth grade
student to graduate from the new Union
School in 1950. That's because he was the
only student in the eighth grade. Union
School is still the smallest grade school in
the state, with a 1990 population of sixty
students, kindergarten through eighth
grade. When the white, wooden two-room
school building opened in 1950, it consolidated the two one-room schoolhouses in
Union, thus ending an era. The school has
since expanded to four rooms. The adults in
the picture are George Olson, principal;
George Graff, superintendent of schools; Ina
Sartorius, school supervisor; The Reverend
Ruth Horsman; Claire Gormley, teacher;
and Ruth Bradway, secretary of the Board of
Education.
Courtesy of Union Historical Society*

Stafford schoolchildren gather for a photograph on the periphery of the classroom. This permits a clear view of the desks that were used. Bolted to the floor, such classroom furniture matched the relatively rigid curriculum that was followed. Courtesy of Stafford Historical Society

Teacher Robert Tongue organized a private school in Tolland in 1890 aft the closing of Tolland Academy, a private secondary school begun in 18? Many academies went out of existence with the advent of town-sponsore secondary schools, but in the case of Tolland, a declining population in t second half of the nineteenth century contributed to its closing. Tongue': school was mainly a preparatory school for those hoping to enter Rockvil High School, which required passing an entrance examination. Since mc students didn't continue their education past eighth grade, those who di had to show they were qualified. The school was held in the Baptist Chur at the north end of the green. Courtesy of Connecticut Historical Society

The parochial school run by St. Mary's Church in Putnam was Notre Dame de Bon Secours Elementary School. Like its name, the school was bilingual. At the time of the photograph, circa 1885, most of the students were French-speaking Canadians, while the nuns, from the order of the Sisters of Mercy, were English-speaking Irish. A language problem persisted even after the nuns were replaced by a French order, the Sisters of the Holy Ghost, since their French wasn't always compatible with the patois of the French-Canadians. Eventually, English became the dominant language of both students and teachers.
Courtesy of Aspinock Historical Society of Putnam

he Hebrew letters printed over the picture of this Yiddish School class spell out the words
'Villimantic School" in Yiddish. The school was run by a local chapter of the Workmen's
'rcle, a national organization of working-class Jews that emphasized the Yiddish language
'd culture rather than religion. At the same time that some of their immigrant parents were
'ing to night school to learn English, these children were preserving the native language of
'eir parents by learning to read and write in Yiddish, a blend of German, Hebrew, and
'ussian. The children, who attended after regular school hours, read Yiddish literature and put
' Yiddish plays in the Noble School auditorium twice a year, where the photograph was taken.
'urtesy of Sarah Axelrod

The town of Columbia sponsored a night school in the 1930s to teach English to newly arrived immigrants, many of whom were Jews who had fled the pogroms and persecution of Eastern Europe. Most of them were already literate in at least three languages — Yiddish, Hebrew, and Russian or Polish. The children of some of them are shown in the Yiddish Sunday School picture. In the back row are the district superintendent of schools and members of the local school committee, including Fannie Dixon Welch, a local politician who promoted the night school. The class was held in the former Moor's Indian Charity School.
Courtesy of Columbia Historical Society

The original Windham High School, built in 1897, is shown here a few years before it burned down in 1913 (see chapter 8). For many years, the high school was the center of secondary education for ma area towns, including Mansfield, Ashford, Andover, Hebron, Hampton, Chaplin, Columbia, Scotland, and Willington. When the new Windham High School was built in 1969, the old building, which replaced this one after the fire, was renovated into the Krame Middle School.
Courtesy of Walter L. Harper

When Prudence Crandall opened a school in this Canterbury house in 1832 exclusively for "young ladies and misses of color," she established the first black female academy in New England. A month later, the Connecticut General Assembly, urged on by some citizens of Canterbury, made it illegal to establish any school for "colored persons who are not inhabitants of this state." Prudence was arrested and found guilty, although she was released on a legal technicality. Meanwhile, the girls at the school were harassed, and an angry mob pelted the building with stones, eggs, and mud. Continuing vandalism forced Prudence to close the school and move west. The building is now maintained as a museum by the Connecticut Historical Commission.
Courtesy of Connecticut Historical Commission, Prudence Crandall Museum

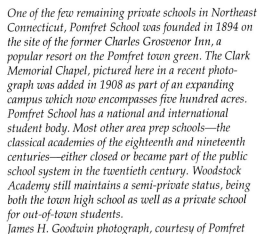

One of the few remaining private schools in Northeast Connecticut, Pomfret School was founded in 1894 on the site of the former Charles Grosvenor Inn, a popular resort on the Pomfret town green. The Clark Memorial Chapel, pictured here in a recent photograph was added in 1908 as part of an expanding campus which now encompasses five hundred acres. Pomfret School has a national and international student body. Most other area prep schools—the classical academies of the eighteenth and nineteenth centuries—either closed or became part of the public school system in the twentieth century. Woodstock Academy still maintains a semi-private status, being both the town high school as well as a private school for out-of-town students.
James H. Goodwin photograph, courtesy of Pomfret School Archives

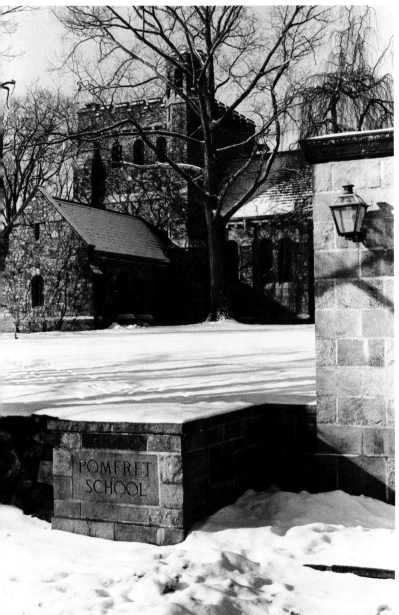

Mansfield Training School, founded in 1917, was the state's largest institution for the mentally retarded, and one of Northeast Connecticut's largest educational facilities. This young boy was one of almost two thousand residents at the institution in the 1960s, all of whom, regardless of age or mental functioning, received some level of schooling or training. Changing attitudes toward the mentally retarded brought about increasing deinstitutionalization, reducing the population at Mansfield to about two hundred residents by 1990.
Courtesy of Mansfield Training School

The athletic programs at Mansfield Training School helped the institution gain a national reputation for excellence. Many of the athletic events were attended by members of the Kennedy family. Here Eunice Kennedy Shriver and world middleweight champion Joey Guardello encourage two young boys prior to a boxing match during a two-day Institute for Physical Education, sponsored by both Mansfield and the University of Connecticut.
Courtesy of Mansfield Training School

The Mansfield Training School Chorus was part of a unique music program that provided music therapy for all of the institution's clients. The chorus, however, was composed of residents who had one unusual feature: they were all blind, as was their director, Gertrude DeLeo, shown seated with her dog, Happy. The Chorus performed solo or with the Training School's Band, playing locally and nationally, including appearances on the "Ed Sullivan Show" and at the New York World's Fair. The group disbanded in the 1970s as its members were placed in community group homes.
Courtesy of Mansfield Training School

Groundbreaking for the Quinebaug Valley Community College in Danielson took place on November 6, 1981. The participants in the ceremony are: State Representative Dorothy Goodwin, Salvatore Morreale, Julia Rankin, Arlene Edmondston, U.S. Representative Sam Gejdensen, Governor William O'Neill, State Representative Kevin Johnston, State Senator Audrey Beck, and Robert E. Miller, founding president of the college.
Courtesy of Quinebaug Valley Community College

Quinebaug Valley Community College—the region's first community college—opened two years later in 1983, providing low-cost higher education for residents of Northeast Connecticut.
Courtesy of Quinebaug Valley Community College

Education kept up with advances in technology and communications so that students were trained in the latest techniques. Here, Aimee Glaude, a communications student at Quinebaug Valley Community College, learns a new craft while participating in a work-study project.
Courtesy of Aimee Glaude and Quinebaug Valley Community College

When the state of Connecticut decided to build a teacher preparation school somewhere in eastern Connecticut, fifty-four Willimantic businessmen and officials held an elaborate banquet for legislators at the Hooker House and offered free land on Valley Street. The General Assembly voted to accept the site in 1889, and the Willimantic Normal School which cost $125,000 was dedicated on May 17, 1895, when this picture was taken. Forty-eight years later, in the early morning hours of August 21, 1943, a fire destroyed the structure and the present building on the same site was dedicated in 1947.
Courtesy of Lucy B. Crosbie and the Willimantic Chronicle

The Willimantic Normal School was one of the first teacher training schools in the country that allowed students to actually teach in a classroom. Their laboratory through the years has been the Noble School, originally known as the Windham Street School. The four teachers-in-training with Grade Two in this 1908 photo are Sara Partrick, Felicia Terry, Josephine Kneeland, and Helene Jacobs.
Courtesy of Archives, Eastern Connecticut State University

Students in a 1903 gymnasium class at the Willimantic Normal School either made their own suits according to prescribed standards, or could have them made to order at the school for about $3.50. Two of the students in the photo have been identified: Lora Whitney Lakin (Brown), extreme left, and Harriette May Little (Kinney), third from left, both Willimantic residents.
Courtesy of Archives, Eastern Connecticut State University

Some members of the Class of 1914 at the Willimantic Normal School pose informally. Sixty-two graduates received diplomas that year, and another eight were awarded certificates.
Courtesy of Archives, Eastern Connecticut State University

The Daisy Chain was already a long-standing tradition by 1928 at the Willimantic Normal School. After members of the junior class picked daisies and made a chain, they would stand in a double row at the steps, and graduating seniors would weave through it at commencement time. *Courtesy of Archives, Eastern Connecticut State University*

A freshman reception in 1957 at the Willimantic State Teachers College shows the increasing proportion of male students at the school. Although the first man enrolled in 1931, forty years after the institution was established, it wasn't until after World War II that men began to enroll in significant numbers. In the 1950s, along with the increase in male students, the overall enrollment more than doubled in size. *Courtesy of Archives, Eastern Connecticut State University*

At Willimantic State College's Reunion Day in 1962, College President J. Eugene Smith posed with alumni, some of whom attended the institution when it was the Willimantic Normal School, a two-year teachers' training school. During the nineteen years of Smith's administration, from 1947 to 1966, the college underwent enormous increases in the size of its campus and student enrollment. Its name change in 1959 to Willimantic State College from Willimantic State Teachers' College reflected its expansion beyond its original teacher training facility. It became Eastern Connecticut State College in 1967, and Eastern Connecticut State University in 1984.
Courtesy of Archives, Eastern Connecticut State University

In 1910, the main campus of the Connecticut Agricultural College consisted of five wooden buildings on "The Hill." They were, from left to right: Grove Cottage, the women's dorm; Gold Hall, the men's dorm; the Main Building; the Chemistry Lab; and the Storrs Experiment Station Office. Classes were held in "Old Main," which also housed a chapel, the president's office, the library, dining room, and the domestic science laboratory. By 1919, three of the buildings had burned down. Old Main was razed in 1929 to make way for Beach Hall. The Experiment Station Office, the only remaining frame building, was moved to another site, where it remained until it was torn down in 1959.
Courtesy of Historical Manuscripts and Archives, University of Connecticut Library

...group portrait of Connecticut Agricultural College's faculty in 1900 ...cludes the institution's first four presidents. They are: Benjamin ...ons, 1881–1898 (second row, center); George W. Flint, 1898–1901 ...ont row, center); Rufus W. Stimson, 1901–1908 (third row, center); ...d Charles L. Beach, 1908–1928 (second row, far left). The college's ...st librarian, Jessie S. Bowen (front row, far right), is also pictured. ...urtesy of Historical Manuscripts and Archives, University of ...nnecticut Library

Students in Connecticut Agricultural College's 1907 Summer School combined a scientific outing with a class picnic at nearby Codfish Falls. The month-long Nature Study course was divided amon, morning classes, afternoon field trips, and evening lectures. Certificate programs were also offered i. Agriculture and Pedagogy, which qualified many Summer School graduates to teach. About one hundred students attended the Summer School each year until the program stopped in 1914. Courtesy of Historical Manuscripts and Archives, University of Connecticut Library

Forestry and Poultry Management classes, were among the earliest courses offered by the Connecticut Agricultural College, and, in fact, are still being offered today. It was unusual in 1907, however, for women to be taking an agricultural course, even one in chicken plucking, since most coeds were enrolled in the Home Economics program. The uniforms worn by the forestry students were necessary attire for the military drills then required of all male students.
Courtesy of Historical Manuscripts and Archives, University of Connecticut Library

The cost of an education at the Connecticut Agricultural College in 1926 was only a fraction of today's prices, especially for this commuting student who didn't even have to pay room and board fees. Like other state residents, he also attended tuition-free. The practice of free tuition for state residents continued until 1972, when a tuition charge of $175 per semester was instituted. Total cost for each semester of the 1990–91 school year, including tuition, room and board, was $3,616.
Courtesy of Historical Manuscripts and Archives, University of Connecticut Library

CONNECTICUT AGRICULTURAL COLLEGE

Garry A.Miles , having paid the prescribed fees, is entitled to the privileges of the College for the semester beginning FEB 3 1926

Matriculation Fee	$5.00
Registration Fee	5.00
Room Rent	37.50
Laboratory Fee	37.50
Tuition	
Breakage Deposit	10.00
Military Deposit	15.00
Athletic Association Fee	7.50
Dining Hall Fee	30.00
	50.00

COMPTROLLER

The "Beanery," or Main Dining Hall, at Connecticut Agricultural College, was built in 1920 to accommodate an increasing student population. Men and women sat at separate tables on opposite sides of the room, and were served by singing waiters. Gradually, dining facilities were incorporated into dormitories, and the Beanery eventually closed.
Courtesy of Historical Manuscripts and Archives, University of Connecticut Library

After a variety of other uses, the old Beanery reopened in 1966 as The William Benton Museum of Art. The museum, recently designated as Connecticut's State Art Museum, maintains a permanent collection, with major holdings in the works of artists Reginald Marsh and Kathe Kollwitz, as well as Tiffany glassworks. It also features changing exhibitions, such as the Mexican Folk Art show, attended here by faculty member and former vice president Kenneth Wilson (right), and Ron and Janet Aronson.
Courtesy of University of Connecticut Photo Services Office

These Italian immigrant railroad workers in Thompson, circa 1915, worked seven days a week, ten hours a day, for a weekly wage of ten dollars. Like other immigrants, they were sometimes discriminated against, and many jobs, including railroad work, weren't always open to them. Samuel Molinaro (top row, left) had to change his name to Sam Miller in order to be hired because, according to his son, "They didn't want Italian names on the payroll." Eventually, Samuel changed his name back to Molinaro. Next to Samuel are Carmine Muraco, and Vincent Molinaro, father of Samuel and Louis, who is seated to the right of two unidentified men. Courtesy of Thompson Historical Society

For many Americans, the mention of New England brings forth images of sturdy Yankees and a landscape dotted with white church steeples rising from architecturally simple and spare houses of worship. While this takes the measure of some of Northeast Connecticut, it misses the rich diversity which shaped the development of Tolland and Windham counties, since the time European settlers collided with Native Americans. On both population and landscape, a variety of ethnic and religious groups left their mark.

Over a century ago, in 1870 shortly after the Civil War, one-fifth of the two counties' population was foreign born; a decade later this edged up to almost a quarter. While immigrants who were Irish born made up a substantial portion of both counties, the ethnic mosaic developed differently with respect to two important groups. More than a quarter of the foreign- born inhabitants of Tolland County had Germanic roots, while only a meager 1 percent of those in Windham did. On the other hand, almost two-thirds of Windham County's foreign born in 1880 came from Canada; in Tolland County, less than 20 percent did. French Canadian textile workers flowed south to work the mills in the extreme eastern part of the state. Proximity to their original home permitted many to be "birds of passage," who traveled back and forth, often on a seasonal basis.

At the same time, in all of Tolland and Windham counties, the census could count only fifteen people born in Italy. The new immigration that brought masses of eastern and southern Europeans to America had not quite started. However, a half century later in 1930, a more pluralistic and diverse population emerged. By that time, America had sharply curtailed immigration through the passage of several restrictive acts at the beginning of the 1920s. Such legislation favored northern and western Europeans, but could not undo the fact that Northeast Connecticut was home to Poles, Italians, Czechs, and Eastern European Jews as well as to those of English, Irish, and German origin. French Canadians still made up more than half of Windham County and 42 percent of the city of Willimantic as the Depression decade began.

A half century later, the contours of the population etched decades before remained. However, new groups appeared among the area's residents. Ukrainians, Hispanics, and Asians reflected the continued transformation of American society. Like immigrants of earlier times their appearance in the locality paralleled broader events of worldwide scope. Wars and economic upheavals worked to shift popula-tions. In the instance of Hispanics primarily Puerto Ricans, many le: their homes on the island to come to the mainland for improved economic conditions. Some used New York City or large Connecti-cut cities as a way station; others flowed directly to jobs in the mill: of Northeast Connecticut. Friend-ship and kinship networks at-tracted an increasing number of migrants, who did not face the obstacles to citizenship that stood before earlier groups. By 1980, the census reported, perhaps underes timating, that more than 1,500 Puerto Ricans resided in Windham County and almost 90 percent of these were residents of the town of Windham, which encompassed the city of Willimantic, site of the American Thread Company.

While blacks had resided in the area since its beginnings, the 1980 census estimated them as only 2 percent of Tolland county's population and 1 percent of Windham's. In fact, the census counted 650 blacks living in Windham county in 1830 and estimated only 512 in 1980. Late into the twentieth century, North east Connecticut remained prima rily an area of white population, although one which was ethni-cally diverse. When the mills, which brought a mixed ethnic population to the area closed thei doors, the people who came to work often stayed, as did their children and their children's children. While the mills were abandoned or readapted to other uses, the meadows remained. More than 60 percent of the population was classified as rural as late as 1980. The character of the area had been set more than a century before when industry developed in the countryside.

The people of Northeast Connecticut brought with them many cultures, values, and attitudes. While some individuals may have been uprooted from their previous homes, they did not lose their old ways but transplanted them. As with all of American society, those who came to reside in the towns of Tolland and Windham counties established familiar institutions while coping with a new environment. Through voluntary associations, benefit societies, athletic clubs, and musical groups, among other means, residents of the northeastern corner of the state made their mark.

For instance, those of German background in Rockville organized a Turnverein, the well-known association, as early as 1858. In 1894, Putnam's St. Jean Baptiste Society, the largest French-Canadian association in New England built a hall, which stood until the 1950s. It became the group's social, cultural, and political center and operated a mutual-aid fund which paid sick and death benefits. A Canadian Athletic Club outfitted a team, which tried to bring glory to the group on the baseball diamond. In Stafford, the Italian Band played its first concert on a Sunday evening in mid-July 1915. In such ways, ethnic groups maintained their identities while faced with the challenges of the American environment.

However, while such activities permitted adjustment through maintenance of old customs, they also separated groups from one another. Discrimination and prejudice did as well, although some condescendingly thought there may be a way out of what they believed to be inherent ethnic inferiority. An observer of Willimantic's Irish wrote in 1885, "When Paddy first lands in the States he is docile and well behaved, although ignorant, as a matter of course. Presently, realizing the breadth and depth of American independence, he kicks up his heels, and, for a time, becomes a useless and almost intolerable member of society. Lastly, finding that, even in America, a fair day's work is required for a fair day's wage, he drops his airs, settles to some

After the mid-nineteenth century, young Irish women flocked to the mills of Northeast Connecticut, followed by French-Canadians, and then waves of other immigrants and inmigrants. These Irish mill girls, circa 1910, resided at The Elms, a boarding house built by the Willimantic Linen Company for its single women employees. The company hired a "missionwoman," who supervised the women's moral progress, whether they were living in The Elms, or in other non-company housing.
Courtesy of Windham Textile and History Museum

useful calling, if, happily, he escapes from keeping a beer-saloon, and, having learned the indispensability of an education he does not himself possess, sends his family to the common school. The children of the first generation improve upon the father and the mother; those of the second are better still; the third can scarcely be distinguished from Americans, and, at Willimantic, examples of every class I have mentioned are working together in the mill."

Ethnic conflict at a variety of levels also was not uncommon. An Irish woman, who had worked in Willimantic's American Thread Company, remembered her youth when Irish and French-Canadian schoolchildren taunted each other

with chants such as, "Corn beef and cabbage make the Irish savage," which met the retort, "Pea soup and Johnny cake makes a Frenchman's belly ache." In the mill, non-French-speaking workers resented use of the French language. As was the case throughout the nation's manufacturing establishments, ethnicity often divided workers. However, within factories, knowing friends or relatives who were in the work force or held supervisory positions, softened the impact of industrialism on ethnics and aided their mobility. This continued to the grave when different groups favored select undertakers and cemeteries. Hence, while immigrant versus Yankee may have

divided the society and culture of Northeast Connecticut, equally sharp divisions occurred among the ethnic groups themselves.

Religious differences intensified such division. The spare Congregational churches that once monopolized New England religion found increasing competition from other Portestant denominations as well as from Catholics and Jews. As the population grew to include new and newer immigrants, they brought their churches and synagogues with them or created new ones. The area's religious institutions became increasingly pluralistic. Yet, traditional religion adhered. For many years, Ashford celebrated the third Wednesday in

ockville's first German social organization was the Turnverein, an athletic club for young
en and women, established in 1857. The Ladies Gymnastics Team, shown in this 1909
iotograph, performed precision drill exercises with their Indian clubs, and competed at the
ite and national level. Besides the Turners, there were fifteen other active German organiza-
ins in Rockville between 1900 and 1920. The Turn Hall, however, was an important
immunity center for the entire town. Its large gymnasium was used for a variety of activities,
cluding strike headquarters during the textile mill strikes of 1919. The building also
ntained a dance hall, restaurant, and saloon. The hall still stands and is now home to the
lish-American Club.
urtesy of Vernon Historical Society

The Saint Jean Baptiste Society Hall, built in 1894, became the center of social, cultural and political activity for French-Canadians who worked in the Putnam mills. Plays, dances, and meetings were held at the hall, located next door to St. Mary's Catholic Church in the French-Canadian section of town near the mills. On the ground floor were a grocery store and meat market, rented out to French-Canadian merchants. The main hall in the building was rented out to other organizations, such as the thirty-family Jewish congregation in Putnam before it had quarters of its own.
Courtesy of Aspinock Historical Society of Putnam

ugust as Bible Day; money ised from activities was used to urchase Bibles for new residents f the town. The Willimantic amp Ground opened at the time f the Civil War. Prayer meetings on many adherents and competi- on among a variety of preachers ade interesting entertainment for e camp's sex segregated partici- ants in the days before other ass entertainment. When Jewish rmers settled in Northeast onnecticut, primarily to work in e chicken and egg business, they ught their own places of wor- ip. In Columbia, the first Jewish rvices were held in someone's

home in 1914; by the mid-1920s, Congregation Agudath Achim built its own synagogue. The small Jewish community of Hebron followed in 1941 by constructing a house of worship in the center of the town. To underline the signifi- cance of the occasion, President Franklin D. Roosevelt sent a letter conveying "his best wishes upon this happy occasion." For all faiths, in more recent times, religion continued to play an important role in the life of North- east Connecticut's people.

Hence, from the time industrial- ism made its impact, a diverse people inhabited Tolland and

Windham counties, an area of twenty-eight towns, all different but with a unity that spelled Northeast Connecticut. Whether immigrant or Yankee, the people of the region contributed to its character by maintaining and modifying old traditions and absorbing new ways.

There was an active chapter of the St. Jean Baptiste Society in
Thompson, as well as Putnam. This parade photograph shows about
20 of its 120 members, all of whom contributed to the building of the
Salle Union, which opened in 1895 in the North Grosvenordale
section of town. Originally a social center for French-Canadian mill
workers, by the 1930s it had become Thompson's first movie theatre
and a social center for the entire town.
Courtesy of Thompson Historical Society

Sports, particularly baseball, provided recreation, camaraderie, and a way of entering American life to many ethnic groups in Northeast Connecticut. These players were members of Putnam's Canadian Athletic Club, circa 1885. They played against the Polish-American Club and the Rumanian Athletic Club, as well as other French-Canadian teams.
Courtesy of Aspinock Historical Society of Putnam

*harles Ethan Porter (second from right) was an African-American artist and Rockville native, who *turned to his hometown after a career in Hartford and New York. He is shown at his Rockville *udio, surrounded by students celebrating his birthday, circa 1911. Porter's achievements—study *d exhibits at the National Academy of Design, travels in France, patronage by Mark Twain and *low artist Frederick Church—were all the more remarkable in light of his humble beginnings as one *nine children of an illiterate laborer. In 1893, he was one of four blacks in the United States singled *t for their achievements in the fine arts. In spite of his recognition, however, Porter never achieved *aterial success. Eventually his work declined, and he ended his days carrying his still-life paintings *or to door in Rockville in exchange for food or flowers to paint.
*urtesy of Ethel Robert

Courtesy of Connecticut Historical Socie

Another side to African-American life in Northeast Connecticut at the turn of the century is revealed in these pictures of unknown bla residents. Not only are the subjects unidentified, but even their location is not always certain. The man by the shanty is thought to from Coventry, the woman shucking corn from Plainfield, and the man mixing mortar from Sterling.

Abraham Krug, a Jewish immigrant, stands on the steps of his White House Cafe lunch wagon, which, in 1920, was located on Willimantic's Union Street, across from the Jillson House. Some immigrant Jews were resettled as farmers through a Jewish philanthropic organization, but others, especially in the larger cities, became merchants.
Courtesy of Lucy B. Crosbie and the Willimantic Chronicle

The shoe repairing shop on Stafford's Main Street was run by F. Carocari, an Italian immigrant. Italians also owned clothing stores in Putnam and fruit stores like Lombardo's in Willimantic.
Courtesy of Stafford Historical Society

Frank P. Lombardo posed with several of his sons and employees in front of his Willimantic Main Street store. Customers agreed that Lombardo's fruits and produce, imported olive oil, cheeses, confections, and tobacco products had no equal.
Courtesy of Lucy B. Crosbie and the Willimantic Chronicle

...is Polish immigrant, known to neighborhood children as "John Wagon," worked as a teamster—literally a ...ver of a team of horses—for the Somersville Manufacturing Company. Like many other Polish and French-...nadian workers at the mill, "John Wagon" never learned to speak English. Recognition of this "tri-lingual" ...iety in certain towns could be seen in World War I Liberty Bond posters that were printed in Polish and French, ...well as English. The photograph is not dated, but it's known to be pre-1931 because the Spiritualist Church in ...background no longer existed after that year.
...rtesy of Somers Historical Society

...dja Jaworsky, who weighed skeins of yarn at the American Thread ...npany, was among a wave of immigrants who worked in the mill ...r World War II. These displaced persons were from Poland, ...many, the Ukraine, Latvia, and Estonia. They were the next-to-... group of immigrant mill workers—the last being Hispanics. This ...ture was taken in 1983, two years before the company closed its ...limantic plant and moved South.
...rtesy of Windham Textile and History Museum

Luisa Mateo, who came to Willimantic from Puerto Rico in 1971, is pictured here in 1977 with her family. The family resided in a West Avenue apartment.
Courtesy of Lucy B. Crosbie and the Willimantic Chronicle

Elder Kent, one of the last ministers of the Advent Society in Abington, poses with his Bible, perhaps pointing to the passage about the Advent, or coming of Christ. The sect was called the Millerites in the mid-nineteenth century after their leader, who, having set the day for the world to come to an end, persuaded many of his followers to dress in white and wait on the roofs of buildings. After a half century of popularity, in part due to several charismatic preachers, membership declined and the church finally closed in 1905, a few years after this photograph was taken. The building was remodeled into a home for the aged and is now the site of the Pomfret Town Office building.
Courtesy of Pomfret Historical Society

Some of these people have just arrived by the trolley at the entrance to the Willimantic Camp Ground. Others came by horse and team. People at the right head up the path to the thirty acres of sloping hillside where annual summer camp meetings have been held for more than 130 years. Similar camp grounds in communities all over the country were part of the Methodist church organization for summer devotional services, featuring outdoor prayer meetings, sermons, and singing. An 1880 description declared the Willimantic Camp Ground as "having every convenience for accommodating the great multitude who annually enjoy its esthetic and spiritual privileges."
Courtesy of Lucy B. Crosbie and the Willimantic Chronicle

The Preacher's Stand at the Willimantic
Camp Ground was surrounded by an
audience circle with a seating capacity for
several thousand people. The summer
religious retreat was so popular that a
special railroad station was built on the site.
Three hundred cottages, as well as a
boarding house, were also built to accommodate guests. About one hundred of the
original buildings are still standing, most of
them winterized for year-round living.
Courtesy of Walter L. Harper

The Ashford Bible Society met once a year
on the third Wednesday in August for a day
of hymns, sermons, and socializing. The goal
of the society was to provide Bibles for
families in the community and to use "kind
persuasion" to influence people to attend
church. The Baptist and Congregational
churches in town took turns hosting the
event, which included a picnic supper and
musical entertainment by a local band. This
photograph was taken in Warrenville on
August 21, 1907, the thirty-sixth annual
Bible meeting.
Courtesy of the Chaplin Museum

The gathering here was the annual May
Festival at the Ellington Congregational
Church, a church-sponsored, town-wide
event. The church was not only the center of
religious and social activities in the town for
many years, it was also its political
headquarters. Until the church burned down
in 1914, both town and grange meetings
were held there, and the selectmen met in its
basement. After the fire, it was decided to
separate town and church, and a Town Hall
was constructed, as well as a new church on
the same site as the old one. Reverend David
Jones, who was pastor from 1898 to 1917, is
in the center holding the dog. Although
undated, the photograph was taken
sometime during the period of his ministry.
Courtesy of Ellington Public Library

Old Trinity Church, the oldest Espiscopal church in Connecticut, was built in 1771 in Brooklyn by Godfrey Malbone, a wealthy dissident Tory. It closed when the Trinity Episcopal Church was built in 1865, but is reopened on special occasions like the annual All Saints' Day observance, shown here in 1947. Evensong services are also held in the old church during August and September.
Courtesy of State Archives, Connecticut State Library

Churches in Northeast Connecticut can be found in busy downtow districts as well as quiet residential neighborhoods. The First Bapti Church in Willimantic stood amidst business establishments like Thread City Candy Kitchen and W. N. Potter's Shoestore in the la nineteenth century. It survived the 1970s urban renewal project ar remains a landmark on Main Street.
Courtesy of Lucy B. Crosbie and the Willimantic Chronicle

The Ebenezer Lutheran Church was organized on November 17, 1889, when "Dan Svenska Evengeliska Lutherska Ebenezerkyrkan av Willimantic" was formed with fifty-four charter members. At the time of this photograph a little girl walks her dog and three children sit on wall of the church. There are no telephone or electric wires to intrude on the view and the dusty dirt road and sidewalks have not yet been paved.
Courtesy of Lucy B. Crosbie and the Willimantic Chronicle

Willimantic's Calvary Baptist Church, established in 1916, was one of the first black congregations in Northeast Connecticut. Its Bank Street location had been the site of Temple B'nai Israel for forty-two years before the synagogue moved outside the downtown area. Previous to that, the building had been a Spiritualist Church and a silent movie theatre. The Calvary Baptist Church bought the synagogue in 1966 before building its own church on Valley Street in 1977—the first black church built in Willimantic.
Frances L. Funk photographs, courtesy of the photographer

This amusing "no parking" sign was displayed at the First Congregational Church in Woodstock. The church, believed to be the oldest in Northeast Connecticut, celebrated its three hundredth anniversary in 1990.
Courtesy of State Archives, Connecticut State Library

Chapter Seven
PLAYING AROUND

This idyllic scene, reminiscent of Tom Sawyer and Huckleberry Finn, is actually a photograph of Earle Pierce and Bill Chase, two Thompson boys at the turn of the century. The pond where they're fishing, now belongs to a local country club. Courtesy of Thompson Historical Society

There is a difference between recreation and rest. When one worked long hours on a farm or in an early factory, little time remained for recreation. One was tired and needed to rest. However, as society modernized, more time for leisure became available. The introduction of machinery reduced drudgery both on farm and in factory. Workers in the nineteenth century advocated an eight-hour day—eight hours for work, eight hours for sleep, and "eight hours for what we will." The final eight allowed people to control their own time and to engage in activities which appealed to them; it permitted a certain kind of self-determination.

Time could be spent on the ball field or the library, in the saloon or in the museum, at the circus or the opera, at the health resort or at the horse races, at the vaudeville show or in the movie house, bicycling or pleasure riding in an auto, billiard playing or bowling, putting or painting. In Northeast Connecticut, as elsewhere in the nation, any number of activities permitted people to pursue their recreational interests as participants or as spectators. They could use their time as they wish and "play around."

Sometimes, however, what seemed to be playing around actually related to matters of health. John Adams' Diary is filled with pages recounting his stay at Stafford Springs in early June 1771. The future president had come on the advice of his doctor to the area discovered by Indian tribes as having curative powers. Rheumatism and skin eruptions reportedly could be cured; vitality would be restored by bathing in and drinking from the magical fluids. In at least one instance, however, Adams, after taking a plunge found the water too cold for a second foray. Nevertheless, the springs became the site of a regional resort and health spa. Dr. Samuel Willard built the first Springs Hotel in 1802. It passed through a number of other owners until a group of business-men formed the Stafford Springs Hotel Corporation in 1894 and opened a new "modern" hotel two years later. Over one thou-sand people attended its opening on February 11, 1896. They celebrated with ice cream, cake, and coffee—a far cry from the acclaimed mineral waters—and danced on the ballroom floor. Sixty-three years later, the build-ing burned down, but the memory of its grandeur and central role in the community did not disappear, although its comforts and poshness were not available to those who could not afford the resort's luxury.

For many, that meant the alternative of relaxing at home. If one was wealthy, the opulence of such an experience could equal, if not surpass, the plushest of resorts. Henry C. Bowen's Roseland Cottage in Woodstock, built as a 22-room summer home in 1842, reflected the newspaper publisher's success and the excess of the era. More modest accommo dations, but no less formal ones, were inhabited by the Arnold family of 812 Main Street in Willimantic (see photos within). At home, middle-class families in the days before radio, TV, VCRs and electronic games would visit with kin, friends, and neighbors, converse, read, make music, and play cards.

While some of the same would occur in the homes, tenements, and apartments of the poor and the working class, less living space and frequently larger families required more activity outside of the residence. Workers' children were more likely to engage in street games, while middle- and upper-class youths could play on their families, large porches or rolling lawns. Adult workers might frequent local saloons such as Young's, later Hebard's, Tavern and Oscar Tanner's Tavern in Willimantic.

The saloon played a central role in the development of communi-ties. For some ethnic groups, it offered a bastion for "bachelor culture" by serving as a meeting place for men; for others, such as German-Americans, it served as a site for family gatherings.

hrough the custom of "treating," the saloon fostered a sense of camaraderie. It often served as a political base for politicians such as Oscar Tanner, mayor of Willimantic for two terms. Overall, the saloon functioned as a place of informality, where the strictures that ruled everyday working life could be overthrown with abandon.

Those desirous of greater culture than provided by the saloon might participate in the Chautauqua movement. It began in Chautauqua, New York, during the 1870s with the goal of uplifting the moral and cultural life of rural communities. By the beginning of the twentieth century, the traveling Chautauqua moved from town to town presenting speakers and entertainment. In the late teens and early twenties during the summer, it played towns such as Vernon and Stafford. On Park Street in Vernon, an audience of several hundred crowded on wooden folding chairs under a circus tent to hear lectures like Russell Conwell's famous paean to the middle class, "Acres of Diamonds." They also listened to concert music and operettas, saw plays, and viewed a number of other events and features. Travelogues were very popular. In 1922, Miss Mildred Clemens, of the Royal Geographical Society, lectured on Happy Hawaii using stereoptican slides and colored moving pictures; moreover, five native Hawaiians sang and danced. For $2.50 an adult was entitled to attend the entire week's two-a-day shows; children paid $1.00, which also included them in several morning programs unavailable to their elders. Even in those days, the price of admission was a bargain.

Vaudeville shows offered another type of amusement. While primarily associated with large cities and the circuits associated with names such as Keith and Albee, the combination of variety show, skits, musicale, and comedy hour was available to the people of Northeast Connecticut. With an emphasis on slapstick humor and ethnic stereotyping, vaudeville appealed to a mass audience both uniting it in laughter and, perhaps, dividing it through such stereotyping. Magicians and escape artists allowed the average person to fantasize flights from their own sometimes difficult surroundings. The precision of the acts and the split-second timing fit well with the factory's clock and the railroad's timetable that overshadowed modern life.

Putnam's Bradley Theatre offered such entertainment during much of the year except the summer when it showed movies; Willimantic's Loomer Opera House provided audiences with live entertainment for fifty-nine years until 1938. In Coventry, vacationing and retired Vaudevillians made their homes around Coventry Lake, attracted to it by entertainers Bill and Mabel Loeser, who had purchased land from another performer and divided it into lots during the 1920s. The neighborhood became known as Actor's Colony. As a private Lake Association, it raised funds for road improvements, not surprisingly, by holding a variety show. A relative of one of the performers remembered years later, "it was nice (for them) to take their old costumes out of the attic."

Vaudeville went out when radio and film came into their own. The movies, first as nickelodeons and then as silent films, appealed to a working class audience. Immigrant workers didn't have to understand English to appreciate film without sound. In 1911, at Putnam's Bradley Theatre, one could see *Buffalo Bill's and Pawnee Bill's Wild West and Far East Shows;* the Star Theater competed with *The White Squaw.* With the advent of talkies, and probably a bit before, movies cultivated a middle-class audience as well.

During the 1920s, film increasingly developed as a mass medium, cutting across all classes of society. Moreover, the architecture of entertainment made movie theatres into special places with names like the Palace or Bijoux. A Willimantic woman remembered back to "the Gem Theatre on Main Street, the Scenic, near the firehouse, and the Capital." With time—and television—such theatres in the region's larger towns were often demolished or converted to other uses. Film going moved to multi-cinema sterile boxes in shopping malls or special movie complexes in redevelopment areas of a town. Moreover, the use of Video Cassette Recorders and Cable TV brought the capacity for moviegoing into the home, adding to its possibilities as an entertainment center, and increasingly privatizing American life.

Attending a vaudeville show or seeing a movie essentially is a passive experience. Residents of Northeast Connecticut recreate in an active fashion as well. They do it indoors and outdoors, as individuals or in groups. They skated on thick and sometimes on thin ice. They joined the bicycling craze when it hit during the late nineteenth century. They participated in "camping out" during the late twentieth century. They took pleasure rides in their automobiles. They might attend a country fair as a spectator, but also could participate by exhibiting livestock or a product, racing a sulky or an auto, or demonstrating a craftsperson's skill. Like the residents of Rockville when the

Warehouse Point trolley started in 1906, they might attend an amusement park such as Piney Ridge, where on the slides and rides individuals took an active role in "playing around." They were more than spectators.

Musical involvement captured the interest of many in the region, whether dancing, singing, or playing an instrument, and reflected active participation in leisure time pursuits. At the turn of the century, Hebron hosted square dancing every Saturday night at the Town Hall; dances in private homes invited "Your company with ladies solicited." Singing societies flourished in Rockville. Prior to 1879, German-Americans organized the Liedertafel. Soon after, residents formed the Singing and Declamation Club. Members of each organization gathered at their group's picnic grove on Sundays for food and songfest. They participated in state and national competitions. Not only did such organizations permit group recreation, but in the instance of those with an ethnic base, they helped preserve native language and provided immigrants with organizing experience. Bands and orchestras allowed the area's residents to pursue their musical bent and Ashford's Town Band reputedly accompanied Knowlton's Rangers to Boston in 1775. In more modern times, brass bands and more general marching bands often stand as the pride of their communities with winners in a "battle of the bands" receiving adulation usually reserved for victorious athletes.

Team sports, of course, offer athletes a chance for local glory.

For the players, there is intense involvement as participants; for fans, there exists the opportunity for total emersion as spectators. Baseball had its roots "in simple, informal folk games played mostly by boys on empty lots of village greens, evolved into a formally organized sport of young gentlemen, and then, within a few decades into a spectator-centered sport." Moreover, many experts contend that General Abner Doubleday had nothing to do with its invention. Whatever Doubleday's role, by 1862 Connecticut had a professional baseball team, the Charter Oaks. Fourteen years later, Hartford became a charter member of the National League. Morgan G. Bulkley, who would serve as the third president of the Aetna Life Insurance Company, mayor of Hartford, governor of Connecticut, and U.S. senator, also initially presided over the League. Connecticut did not stay in the Majors for long, being caught between the New York and Boston metropolises. However, it has remained actively involved at the Minor League level.

Semi-pro, local and school teams abounded. Columbia laid out a baseball diamond on its green in 1875. Dr. Julian LaPierre organized, managed, scheduled, and umpired for its first team, which played opponents from Coventry, Lebanon, Hebron, and Gilead. By the 1880s, a black youth, John Richards, led the team and earned a reputation as the best all-around player of his time. Willimantic served as home for formally organized teams during the same period. In 1887, Putnam residents closely followed the

rivalry between Danielson and Attawaugan. Hence, from an early era, residents of Northeast Connecticut pursued the national pastime, which in recent times has been distinguished by play at Eastern Connecticut State University. Baseball, played on fields, celebrated rural America; games, divided in innings and drowning in statistics, tried to make efficient use of time and celebrated modern society. By combining the two, it is not difficult to see the game's appeal to the region and the nation and why contemporary Little Leagues follow in a long tradition.

Other team sports drew their adherents. Especially at the high school and college level, football and basketball and later soccer developed a wide audience as well as many active participants. While Yale dominated Connecticut college football from its initial contests in the late nineteenth century, in recent years the University of Connecticut from Storrs has been its match. Moreover, basketball fans throughout the state and nation focus upon the northeastern region every time the Huskies play a game. With membership in the Big East Conference and memories of the victorious 1989-90 season, basketball in the quiet corner is anything but quiet.

Playing around, then, takes many forms and the use of leisure time has become serious business in our mass culture. The choices for recreation multiply exponentially with the passing of each year. Whether participant or spectator, player or fan, the use of one's free time is filled with variety but is not always relaxing.

Leisure for the wealthy in the nineteenth century often meant a summer home in the country. Roseland Cottage in Woodstock, a twenty-two room Gothic Revival house, was built in 1842 for Henry C. Bowen, a newspaper publisher and former Woodstock native. Bowen hosted gala Fourth of July celebrations at Roseland Cottage, where he entertained prominent political figures, including Presidents Grant, Hayes, Harrison, and McKinley. One of the country's earliest bowling alleys was built on the property for Bowen and his guests. Constance Holt, a granddaughter of Bowen, shown here in the parterre garden, circa 1904, spent summers at the cottage until she died in 1968. The property, now open to the public, is also called Bowen House, or Pink House, a tribute to its vividly colored facade.
Courtesy of SPNEA Archives

he Stafford Springs House was one of the rgest of many resort hotels in Northeast onnecticut in the nineteenth and early ventieth centuries. It was built on the site of a ineral springs famous since Indian days. The urative powers of the water drew colonists, too, cluding John Adams who rode there on orseback from Boston in 1771. Various uesthouses put up early visitors, but it wasn't ntil 1802 that a luxury hotel was built, and the wn became a spa comparable to Poland orings, Maine, or Saratoga Springs, New ork. In 1896, the old hotel was torn down and new one, shown in the photo, was constructed. continued to be a focal point of the town until fire in 1959 destroyed this historic landmark. ourtesy of Stafford Historical Society

Despite billiards' original popularity in gentlemen's clubs, the game is not always played in the most genteel neighborhoods. This billiard room in Moosup opened at 3 p.m. on weekdays and 1 p.m. on weekends; it stayed open until 10 p.m.
Lee Jacobus photograph, courtesy of the photographer

This photo of the Tennis Club of Rockville was taken on July 27, 1889. Imagine women having to play in the long dresses and the consequent slower game.
Courtesy of Vernon Historical Society

Reading aloud was a pastime in the late nineteenth century. In this 1895 photo, Ellen Larned, a noted Windham County historian from Thompson, is reading a historical paper to an assorted group of listeners, some of whom seem to be taking time out from other leisure-time activities.
Courtesy of Thompson Historical Society

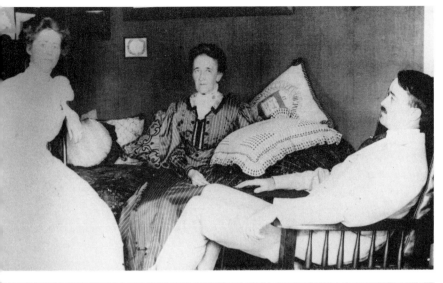

The Arnold family of Willimantic posed for a quiet evening at home. Mrs. Ansel Arnold, lived with her daughter and son William, a judge of the local police court. Family pictures and handworked fancy pillows, one of them bearing a collegiate seal, conjure up an era of unhurried pastimes.
Courtesy of Lucy B. Crosbie and the Willimantic Chronicle

Touring plays and vaudeville shows were popular entertainment at the Bradley Theatre in Putnam. When movies appeared in the early twentieth century, they were usually a summertime-only event, with a return to live entertainment in the fall. Many of the old theatres and opera houses in the area have been torn down or renovated for other uses, but the Bradley Playhouse has been restored into a non-profit, community-based theatre that runs a year-round operation of concerts, plays, and children's theatre.
Courtesy of Walter L. Harper

This Main Street billboard in Willimantic advertised the appearance of James Thatcher as Quincy Adams Sawyer appearing for one night only at the Loomer Opera House. Traveling and local theatrical groups performed on the 40-by-60-foot stage of the 1,100-seat theatre for fifty-nine years until the building was razed in 1938 to make way for the F.W. Woolworth building.
Courtesy of Lucy B. Crosbie and the Willimantic Chronicle.

Bicycling became a national fad during the late nineteenth century and the town of Vernon was no exception to its attraction. For many, however, it was not a fad. It was a means of transportation. Note the formal pose and dress of those involved in this leisure-time activity. Courtesy of Vernon Historical Society

Willimantic's Thread City Cyclers, crack riders all, fresh from their victory over a Norwich team, posed for this studio portrait in 1893. In the back row are James Hurley, Dr. George E. Wilcox, Charles B. Newton, Irvin G. Bissell, and Lewis L. Keigwin. Seated are William P. Jorday, George E. Hinman (later Attorney General and a justice of the Connecticut Supreme Court). George A. Bartlett holds the leash of future Mayor Daniel P. Dunn's English bulldog Billie, the cyclers' mascot. The invention of the safety bicycle with wheels of equal size brought thousands of men and women out onto the roads and into the countryside. According to the 1900 census, "few articles ever used by men have caused so great a revolution in social conditions as the bicycle." The bicycle remained a popular mode of transportation until the 1920s when the automobile took over, but its recreational popularity has continued to the present day. Courtesy of Lucy B. Crosbie and the Willimantic Chronicle

The Eastford Bicycle Club, circa 1900, pose in front of the Eastford House, which later became known as the General Lyon Inn. The young women in the club are Florence Warren, Mabel Converse, and Mary Keith. The young men are Charles Tatem, William Warren, and Charlie Johnson, and the small boy is Dana Keith.
Courtesy of Eastford Historical Society

Ice skating on Swan Lake was a popular winter activity at the Connecticut Agricultural College at the turn of the century, as were dances and taffy pulls. Warm weather social events included picnicking, fishing, and "other delightful jaunts," according to the student newspaper. The newspaper complained, however, that "the chaperones are always with us." The Storrs Congregational Church in the background was the predecessor of the current building, which replaced it in 1929. The earlier structure faced Route 195, rather than North Eagleville Road, as the church does now.
Courtesy of Historical Manuscripts and Archives, University of Connecticut Library

Pleasure boaters aboard the Captain Nathan Hale on Coventry's Lake Wangumbaug are watched by onlookers at the boat launch. Nathan Hale's Homestead is not far from the lake, which for many years has attracted vacationers to the town.
Courtesy of Walter L. Harper

Mashamoquet Brook State Park is one of several state parks and forests in wooded Northeast Connecticut. Located in the Abington section of Pomfret, it contains over eight hundred acres reserved for swimming, camping, and fishing. Part of the park includes a trail to Wolf Den, where Revolutionary War General Israel Putnam is said to have slain the last wolf in Connecticut. *Courtesy of Walter L. Harper*

In the lazy days of summers long gone by, Lake Wangumbaug, known as Coventry Lake, was a popular bathing and boating place when photographer Julian Beville took this picture titled Tourist Camp. Trolley excursions carried thousands to the Lakeside Casino for boating, dancing, and picnics. Another location at the lake, called Girard Park, became known as the Actors' Colony when a number of vaudeville, stage, and radio stars built summer homes here in the late 1920's.
Courtesy of Lucy B. Crosbie and the Willimantic Chronicle

Photographer E. P. Rose captured the pleasures of camping and fishing on the Natchaug River in Mansfield in this turn-of-the-century photograph. The tent, clothes drying on the line, and the presence of cooking seem to indicate that the men were staying for a day or two to fish, swap stories, and seek relief from the hustle and bustle of nearby Willimantic only a few miles away from this tranquil setting.
Courtesy of Lucy B. Crosbie and the Willimantic Chronicle

Brass bands provided rousing, patriotic entertainment at the turn of the century. Every town had at least one, and most likely several, organized by churches, ethnic societies, civic groups, or individuals. They performed in bandstands on town greens, marched in parades, and, on Memorial Day, traveled to town cemeteries to pay respect to fallen soldiers. Charles N. C. Wheeler, standing over the drum in the center of this gathering, organized both boys' and adult bands. The present-day Windham Concert Band descends from Wheeler's bands.
Courtesy of Edward Gerry

Less formal musical groups, known as "rag-tag" bands, might have played local dance halls and theatres. They were more eclectic, generally, with young and older members, as well as native and foreign-born, although many immigrant groups formed their own bands.
Courtesy of Edward Gerry

The reed instrumentalists in this 1927 Putnam photograph are shown with their teacher, Adolph Bernier (third from left, second row). Private music lessons were commonplace before schools began teaching instrumental music. Bernier's students, who paid fifty cents for an hour's lesson, played in local marching bands or little orchestras.
Courtesy of Aspinock Historical Society of Putnam

143

Baseball was still an informal affair in 1896 at the Storrs Agricultural College. Games were mostly intramural, pitting the seniors against other classes, or with neighboring town leagues like Eaglevil or Willimantic. Occasionally, a team traveled to another school, such as the Rhode Island Agricultural College, or competed against the alumni on commencement day.
Courtesy of Historical Manuscripts and Archives, University of Connecticut Library

The orange-jerseyed "Aggies" of the Connecticut Agricultural College were heavy favorites to win against Springfield in October 1927, but overconfidence may have contributed to their 31-21 defeat. The student newspaper editorialized: "Perhaps Springfield's offence [sic] looked good because of the Aggies' weak defense." The school's athletic teams were called "Aggies" until 1933, when Connecticut Agricultural College became Connecticut State College, and the teams adopted the nickname "Huskies."
Courtesy of Historical Manuscripts and Archives, University of Connecticut Library

...nneth Wright, No. 31, goes to the top of the basket as leading scorer ...ny Hanson, No. 25, looks on during a game with East Carolina on ...nuary 11, 1975. The final score was 79-77 in favor of the Huskies. ...urtesy of Historical Manuscripts and Archives, University of ...nnecticut Library

UConn's Tate George takes charge against St. John's during the basketball team's debut at the opening of the Gampel Pavilion on the Storrs campus, January 27, 1990. Later in the season, George would sink "the shot" to beat Clemson in the final second of their game in the NCAA Tournament and the penultimate game of UConn's "Dream Season."
Courtesy of University of Connecticut Photo Services Office

These remarkable photographs of the collapsing steeple of Willimantic's First Congregational Church were taken at the height of the 1938 hurricane by John McDonald, an amateur photographer. McDonald used a borrowed box camera and split-second timing to take these photos from the doorway of a building two blocks away. He later sold the pictures to Life Magazine. Courtesy of John McDonald

Chapter Eight
THE SKY IS FALLING

Disaster! Disaster, a simple word which instills fear and raises goose pimples. Fire, flood, blizzard, bring forth images of Biblical wrath. Train and auto crashes add a man-made dimension to the apocalypse. All leave an indelible impression on the collective memory of a community. To this, Northeast Connecticut is no exception. While it has had no Chicago Fire or San Francisco Earthquake, events deeply etched in the nation's consciousness, like any other region, the quiet corner has had its share of disastrous events. Just as such events and the response to them reflected vulnerability but also capacity for renewal, the people of the towns of Tolland and Windham counties have rebounded from adversity.

From the beginning of New England settlement, Indians and later white colonists had to contend with the area's cantankerous weather. Long, harsh winters left many feeling stranded. During the 1640s, one settler remarked, "You must looke upon us as prisoners from the end of 9ber [September] till the beginning of Aprille." More than two centuries later, that famous Hartfordite, Mark Twain, described the region's "sumptuous variety" of weather as "probable nor'east to sou'west winds, varying to the southard and westard and eastard and points

between; high and low barometer sweeping round from place to place; probably areas of rain, snow, hail, and drought, succeeded or preceded by earthquake with thunder and lightening." What matter did it make anyway? As the noted author reputedly pointed out, everyone talks about the weather but no one does anything about it!

Its variety, however, certainly provided the opportunity for response. Vernon's citizens found this to be the case in 1869 when it rained torrents on the first Sunday and Monday of October. Lakes, ponds, and streams overflowed, taking with them bridges and moveable property as well as eroding embankments. Mills in Talcottville and Rockville suffered severe damage; railroad tracks drowned under water. Dams burst. Roads separated. An impassable gulf of twenty to thirty feet extended across Tolland Avenue. Without modern equipment, using only horses, oxen, and hand tools, it took residents months to make roads again passable and to complete repairs generally.

Vernon's freshet of 1869 pales in historical memory and impact compared to the famed Blizzard of '88. From Monday through Wednesday, March 12-14, 1888, it snowed and snowed and snowed. One estimate measured two feet in Putnam; another counted three

feet in Hebron with drifts as high as twenty feet. There the lore of the storm claims that residents "burrowed" their way to "outhouses"—the only reason anyone went outside. Mills in Putnam suspended operations because the dense snow impeded the flow of water to power them. Trains stalled. On Monday, the Limited Express passed through that town but didn't reach Willimantic until Tuesday; it had stalled in Hampton. Tragedy struck when two persons on a farm near Pomfret Landing froze to death and were not discovered for a week. Their dinner of wheat, bread, and buckwheat remained uneaten on the kitchen table.

However, as with any event, some individuals overcame their circumstances; others have positive experiences despite the adverse situation. Large gangs of workers labored without modern equipment to clear roadways quickly and by the next week nature helped in evaporating the snow, although remnants of the Blizzard remained long after. For one Willimantic man, nature's snowy excess shaped his future. Marooned in the Turnerville section of Hebron with a young woman he just met, the new relationship blossomed into marriage.

A half-century later in 1938, another memorable natural disaster struck. "The New En-land Express," the first tropical hurricane to visit the region since 1815, hit Connecticut on Wednesday, September 21. The storm was a killer. In all of the New England states, 682 people died; 700 were injured. Eighty-five Connecticut residents lost their lives. Damage was extensive. According to the Hartford Courant, the day was the "most calamitous" in the state's history to that time. The fact that the weather bureau failed to give warning of the storm's true potential made the devastation all the worse.

In Stafford, the hurricane struck with greatest intensity at four o'clock in the afternoon and raged for two hours. While there were no fatalities, falling trees and branches and flying roof shingles made for many narrow escapes. Residents cowered in their homes. One woman recalled watching with frozen fascination "the flying bricks from a neighbor's chimney, swirling cabbage leaves from the garden and the apple trees in the fields toppling over like wooden soldiers. It was an afternoon of terror." In Willimantic, church steeples toppled and cars were smashed (see photographs within). In Ashford, temporary food shortages plagued the community, which thought itself self-sufficient. Putnam was one of the hardest hit communities in the state. There, buildings were ripped from their foundations; railroad sheds crumbled into heaps; the Congregational Church lost its steeple; the Providence Street railroad bridge collapsed. Flood levels were unprecedented. Three died and five hundred found themselves homeless. Martial law had to be declared and the National Guard patrolled. Because of the devastation, all residents were mobilized in the cleanup. As one wrote in his diary, "Every man in Putnam had a job as long as he had an axe."

Another hurricane, "Diane," caused some of the worst flooding in Connecticut's history when it hit in August 1955; the state bore two-thirds of the $700,000,000 damage cost to all of New England. Again, Putnam, among the towns of the northeastern corner, suffered dramatically. The Quinebaug and French rivers inundated the city, making the destruction of 1938 pale in comparison. Factories suffered as if made of children's building blocks. Explosion, fire, collapse accompanied the sweeping currents of water. One old mill stood "tilted at a 45 degree angle toward the eastern shore." The city's three bridges were destroyed along with the New Haven railroad trestle. Its new, but still unoccupied library, swam in five feet of water on its first floor. Eleven people spent a trying night stranded on top of the state garage behind Main Street. The city's mayor, John N. Dempsey, who became Connecticut's governor, remembered that Putnam's citizens rose to the situation. "They accepted the challenge and they built a better place in which to live."

In Stafford, too, the floods caused by Diane took a toll greater than the damage of 1938. When the Rhode Island mill dam burst, waters from the Middle River rampaged through the western part of the town. Further to the south and east of the quiet corner, at Wauregan Mills in Plainfield, the floods took their toll on a declining industry. Fourteen feet of water filled sections of the mill and devastated equipment (see photograph). Four years later the plant closed, in part weighed down by the cost of replacement machines, in part following the general trend affecting New England textile manufacture. In this instance, the effects of nature's impact were not easily overcome,

particularly when so many man-made signs pointed to the textile industry's regional demise.

Nature has taken its toll in more recent years in the ice storm of 1973, the Blizzard of 1978, and a variety of storms during the 1980s. However, snow, ice, hurricane, and flood alone do not threaten humankind. Every town in the northeastern corner has suffered from its share of fires. While not of the magnitude of the conflagrations in Chicago in 1871, Boston in 1872, and Baltimore in 1904, which offered residents of those cities the opportunity to improve their inadequately built cities, fires in Northeast Connecticut have presented challenges to which the twenty-eight towns in Tolland and Windham counties have responded. However, even in the large metropolises limits existed to the power to improve buildings and infrastructures and spatial patterns.

While a phoenix-like rising from the ashes of damaging fires is not always possible, coping with such disaster gave rise to a major community resource of the region. Volunteer fire departments play not only an important public safety role in the area's towns, but a social one as well. The fire houses that shelter them serve as gathering places and points of town esprit and camaraderie. Windham Center's Volunteer Department dates back as far as 1824; South Windham's was organized in 1911 and North Windham's in 1926. In Willington, the No. 1 Fire Department formed in 1941 and the No. 2 incorporated in 1952. Sometimes, departments factionalize as happened in Tolland around 1930 and two competing groups arise; sometimes volunteers organized because the needs of different parts of a town demanded it and then engage in friendly competition.

Fortunately for the residents of

Northeast Connecticut, they avoided a practice that occurred in large cities during the early nineteenth century. Then, volunteers from different neighborhoods often fought with each other for the honor to still a fire. While the fights raged, so did the flames!

Modernization and technological innovation brought other possibilities for disaster. With the expansion of railroad traffic during the late nineteenth century, accidents were not uncommon. During the early 1890s, coming around a station curve in East Thompson, fast freight No. 202 met the Southbridge Local head on. The early morning air shattered with the crash; steel and wood flew on to adjacent tracks; fire erupted. At 6:47 a.m. (the time on the dead engineer's smashed pocket watch), the Eastern States Express barreled around the curve at fifty miles per hour and smashed into the debris on Track 2. It derailed and did a 180 degree turn, killing two. To add to the tragedy, the Norwich Boat train rear-ended the Express. Not long after, a spectacular wreck occurred in December 1896 on the Central Vermont when engine No. 155's boiler exploded while passing through Mansfield. Mass transit within towns did not escape such problems as trolleys grew in popularity. Witness within the photograph of the wreck on December 2, 1909. Needless to say, the automobile brought with a potential to move quickly, sometimes too quickly with tragic end. Hence, the possibility for disaster in life, individual and community-based, is infinite. Fortunately, the ability of human beings to cope and to survive, to achieve beyond adversity and to renew, is equally strong. The people of Northeast Connecticut have demonstrated this.

The Great Blizzard of 1888 raged for three days across Northeast Connecticut, as it did throughout the northeastern United States. When it finally stopped, people gathered, as here on Stafford's Main Street, to talk about it and/or shovel. It took days of shoveling to get trains running and communications restored. Many factories in the area closed because the heavy snow impeded the flow of water to them, and idle mill workers joined town crews in the monumental task of digging out.
Courtesy of Stafford Historical Society

The twentieth century's reliance on the automobile made the Blizzard of 1978 even more crippling than the storm ninety years earlier. Even if this car in Willimantic had been dug out, it would still be immobilized, as roads remained impassable for days, and highways were banned to all but emergency vehicles. Sophisticated snowplowing equipment wasn't any more effective than old-fashioned shovels in the face of constantly shifting drifts.
Harold Hanka photograph, courtesy of the photographer

Four days of steady rain preceded the hurricane of 1938, causing extensive flooding in Willimantic. These scenes of Bridge Street show the overflowing Willimantic River submerging the street and railroad tracks, isolating the area from the rest of the city. Three young men narrowly escaped drowning when they and the car they were pushing were swept down an embankment by the surging current. Rescuers threw them a rope and pulled them to safety as the car washed away.
John McDonald photographs, courtesy of the photographer

Astonished Willimantic residents surveyed the damage in the aftermath of the 1938 hurricane. A car parked next to the Town Hall was crushed when part of the building's roof collapsed on it during the height of the storm. The owner of the brand-new car, Frank Oliver, was a telephone company employee who worked across the street from the Town Hall. Given the intensity and unexpectedness of the hurricane, it was remarkable that only one person was killed in Willimantic, although many dozens were injured.
Courtesy of John McDonald

In the 100-mile-per-hour winds of the 1938 hurricane, buildings were ripped from their foundations. This toppled structure was on Willowbrook Street near Route 6 in Willimantic. The destruction caused by the hurricane had one positive effect: it virtually eliminated the unemployment problems in Northeast Connecticut, since all available manpower was mobilized for the massive cleanup.
Courtesy of John McDonald

Ellis Howard, a Wauregan Mills worker, prepared for Hurricane Diane on August 18, 1955, by moving bales of Egyptian cotton out of the warehouse in anticipation of high water. In spite of his efforts, three hundred bales were swept away down the Quinebaug River, but all but one were eventually recovered. Because the bales were so highly compressed, only 10 percent of the material was lost.
Courtesy of Historical Manuscripts and Archives, University of Connecticut Library

The floods that followed Hurricane Diane in August 1955 ravaged equipment in the basement spinning room of Wauregan Mills in Plainfield. In parts of the mill the water rose to fourteen feet. Although the mill remained open for four more years after used equipment was installed, the expense created by the flood led to the mill's closing a few years later.
Courtesy of Historical Manuscripts and Archives, University of Connecticut Library

The Hilltop Hose apparatus is still at the scene the morning after the November 22, 1916 fire at the Jordan Hardware Company in Willimantic. Spectators viewing the damage were unaware that even more destruction was to follow. Two days later, people assembled again to watch the demolition of the building considered to be unsafe after the fire. Sixty pounds of dynamite were used, and after the smoke and dust cleared, scores of spectators had been injured by the blast; one man later died of his injuries. A large granite boulder was hurled hundreds of feet passing right through a moving railroad car filled with passengers, and a brakeman walking along the tracks had his clothes blown off. The subsequent court trial found that the amount of dynamite was "excessive and dangerous."
Courtesy of Lucy B. Crosbie and the Willimantic Chronicle

A fire which began in the hayloft of a Stafford livery stable in 1917 burned down the stable and destroyed the Baker Block, which included the 109-year-old Baker Furniture Company. Extraordinar efforts by firemen saved the adjacent First National Bank building, "the most important building in the city," according to a newspape account. The building included the town clerk's office and the Masonic Hall.
Courtesy of Stafford Historical Society

When 94-year-old Harriet Bass Fenton walked downtown from her home on upper Church Street in Willimantic to see what the commotion was all about at Lincoln (now Jillson) Square, she was quite nonplussed to find herself at the scene of the disastrous Valentine's Day fire of February 14-15, 1968. The fire, which destroyed several buildings between the First Baptist Church and Church Street in Willimantic, raged for nearly twenty-four hours fueled by 25,000 gallons of paint from the store where it started.
Courtesy of Lucy B. Crosbie and the Willimantic Chronicle

154

The firemen battling the blaze which burned down the popular Shell Chateau restaurant in
Willimantic in July 1979 were too busy to notice the sign next door, but its irony didn't
escape the photographer.
Harold Hanka photograph, courtesy of the photographer

Courtesy of Lucy B. Crosbie and the Willimantic Chronicle   Courtesy of Stafford Historical Society

Train and trolley wrecks were spectacular events, often drawing crew, passengers, and
onlookers to pose amid the wreckage. The train accident took place in Stafford, although the
date and circumstances are unknown. The trolley accident occurred in South Windham in
1909. According to a newspaper account, it jumped the tracks at the end of a steep grade and
went down into a fifteen-foot ditch. Both trains and trolleys had "cow-catching" grates in
front that pushed aside animals that strayed onto the tracks, a source of many accidents.

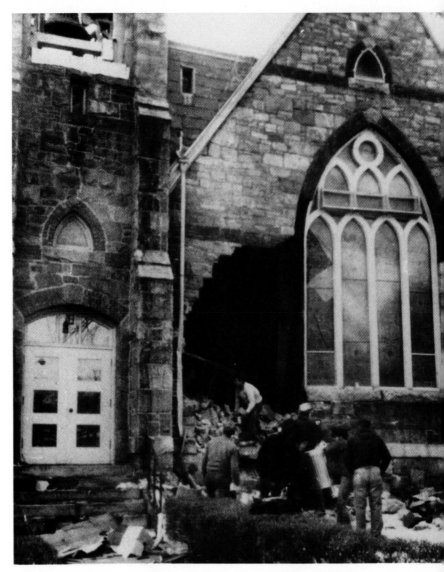

Area churches have withstood their share of damage from hurricanes, fires, and floods, but the Stafford Springs Congregational Church may be the only one ever hit by a truck. On the morning of May 10, 1969, a tractor-trailer carrying five tons of coffee smashed through the Main Street stone church. The driver was injured but fortunately no one was in the church at the time. Besides the hole in the church, the steeple was damaged from the impact of the crash.
Courtesy of Stafford Historical Society

The hurricane of 1938 caused extensive damage to St. Joseph's Church in Willimantic, as it did to many other churches in Northeast Connecticut. The crashing steeple tore a large hole in the roof of the church and destroyed much of the brick tower beneath it.
Courtesy of John McDonald

Most of the repairs to St. Joseph's Church were completed by 1954, but it wasn't until 1989, nearly fifty-one years after the hurricane, that the steeple itself was finally replaced. The new steeple, shown here being installed, is made of aluminum and designed to withstand winds up to 130 miles an hour. Frances L. Funk photograph, courtesy of the photographer

Co. E   1898
Corner Valley and Highst
Willimantic

Chapter Nine
WAR AND COMMUNITY

*One hundred and fifteen men who left Willimantic to serve in Company E, Third Regiment,
Connecticut Infantry, U.S. Volunteers, posed at the corner of Valley and High streets before leaving
for the Spanish-American War in 1898. When a mysterious explosion sent the U.S. Battleship
Maine to the bottom of Havana harbor in an incident that contributed to the outbreak of that war,
one of the victims was Patrick J. Shea of Willimantic, a first-class fireman coal-passer on the ship.
Courtesy of Lucy B. Crosbie and the* Willimantic Chronicle

Wars are fought on the warfront and the homefront. For the past century, these have been different places for the United States. Prior to that time, the distinction was less clear. Wars change society and affect communities. Communities usually support the war effort, but sometimes individuals within them do not. As a result, tensions arise between individual rights and community needs, between liberty and security, between government and citizen, and between differing views of patriotism. In Northeast Connecticut, as in the rest of the nation, cohesion and division have vied during wartime, but always the region has contributed to America's effort.

Connecticut's first military foray, the Pequot War of 1637, ended in Indian extermination unjustified by the Pequot threat. Throughout the colonial period, the colony's fate was entwined with the struggle between England and France and the relationship to the area's first settlers. Military action was not uncommon. During the French and Indian War, which festered between 1754 and 1763, Connecticut raised twenty thousand troops — one of every five of its men. It also performed yeoman's service in provisioning the British troops, proportionally spending more than any other colony.

When the colonies and Britain tangled in the events leading to the Revolution, Connecticut played a major role as it did during the actual war itself. Its citizens made up sixteen of George Washington's regiments and individuals such as Israel Putnam of Pomfret, Thomas Knowlton of Ashford, and Benedict Arnold (not yet known as a traitor) played leading roles in the war effort. Connecticut continued its role of chief supplier and, with two of its residents serving as commissary-generals of the Army, earned the name "the Provisions State." When the British closed the port of Boston in 1774, towns in Northeast Connecticut responded. Windham sent to Boston more than 250 sheep and Pomfret 105 to help relieve the resulting food shortages. Union contributed four hundred pounds of black lead from one of its mines for use in the manufacture of cannons for the American forces. Women contributed by taking over farm work when men left for battle.

However, not everyone supported the Revolution. Tories, like Hebron's Angelican minister, the Reverend Samuel Peters, saw things differently from those who later would be honored as American patriots. When Hebron turned down Connecticut Governor Trumbull's request to assist the people of Boston at the time of the blockade, the Governor encour-aged opposition to the clergyman. On August 14, 1774, a crowd from Windham marched on Peter's house, arriving at midnight, to search for seditious papers, but found none and left. Later, another mob led by the Governor's son attempted to have the minister sign a loyalty oath to America. Peters refused. The crowd, some of whom were inebriated, stripped him of all but his breeches and yelled names and bellowed charges. Then, he was carried off, and threatened with tarring, feathering, and being hung by his hands. Some Hebron townspeople came to his rescue and soon after the Reverend sailed for London, where he wrote the General History of Connecticut, published in 1781. Not surprisingly, Peters stressed the narrow puritanical code which stifled dissent. Once the nation was established, during the War of 1812, the entire state reluctantly participated in what Federalist Connecticut saw as a Jeffersonian adventure. In 1814, at the Old State House, the Hartford Convention drafted anti-war resolutions. Nor did anti-slavery Connecticut give strong support to the Mexican War of 1848. On the other hand, the state vigorously contributed to the Union's victory in the Civil War.

Not only did 55,000 men serve but 20,000 died, were wounded, or were listed as missing in action. The Irish contributed regiments

mposed of 7,900 soldiers; two
ack regiments fought. On home
rritory, Colt's and Sharp's in
artford and Winchester Arms in
ew Haven produced weapons in
rge numbers; Mystic's shipyards
unched fifty-six steamers for the
avy. In Northeast Connecticut
e textile industry contributed to
e war effort as did other manu-
cturers. Mansfield's Eagle
anufacturing Company, located
the Eagleville section, received
government contract to manu-
cture twenty-five thousand
mpression rifle muskets. Towns-
eople showed concern at the
tbreak of the war when twenty-
e petitioned to call a town
eeting "for the purpose of taking
tion relative to the present
tuation of the affairs of the
untry, and the duties of said
wn of Mansfield relating to the
me." Although the next week
e town meeting apparently
etermined to leave matters to the
ate legislature, like many other
mmunities, Mansfield pro-
eded to offer bounties to those
ho would serve in the military.
e bounties could be used to buy
substitute, a practice common at
e time. The town even ap-
ointed an agent, Simeon O.
inton, to raise volunteers to fill
quota for soldiers; he received
to $100 for each man recruited.
Ashford and Putnam, area
sidents aided runaway slaves
a the "underground railroad."
esidents of the latter town hid
aves in a secret cell in the former
asonic building, which served as
"station" on the route to Canada.
volvement in the Civil War,
ught on American territory,
uld not be escaped.

By the late nineteenth century,
merica looked outward and its
ars no longer would be fought
home territory, although the
omefront would be dramatically
fected during wartime in the
ventieth century. During the

Spanish-American War of 1898,
the United States joined the
world's expansionist powers.
Victory came quickly and, afterwards, America controlled the
Philippines, Puerto Rico, and, less
directly, Cuba as well as other
territory. The sun never set on the
American Empire. Connecticut's
regiments responding to President
McKinley's call spent the war at
Niantic or in Maine or Virginia,
although about 3,400 volunteers
saw active duty; only those in
regular service prior to the "Splen-
did Little War," as it was dubbed
by Secretary of State John Hay,
saw combat. This benefitted not at
all the sailor from Willimantic
killed by the explosion on the
battleship Maine in Havana
Harbor, which sparked America's
entrance into the war. That explosion, by the way, more than likely
resulted from an erupting boiler
rather than any Spanish sabotage,
although the cause mattered little
to the grieving family and friends
in Northeast Connecticut, who
always would "Remember the
Maine!"

The Great War, for obvious
reasons not yet called World War
I, broke out in Europe in 1914, but
the United States did not enter
until three years later. Prior to that
time, in 1916, President Woodrow
Wilson called up 150,000 militia to
be stationed along the Mexican
border as a warning to Pancho
Villa, who killed Americans on
both sides of it. On June 24, 1916,
eight thousand people in
Willimantic watched the seventy-
three men and three commissioned officers of Company L go
off to service. A newspaper
reported, "The scene was not
without its element of sadness.
There were many tears shed.
Mothers, wives, sisters, sweet-
hearts crying, were everywhere
seen. Even the stronger ones, such
as fathers and brothers, had
moistened eyes. It was a scene that

will long be remembered." Mayor
Daniel P. Dunn, carrying a big
flag, expressed the hope that all
would return safely and that as
noble sons of Windham they
would be bold and strong in the
tradition of earlier area servicemen. While the troops ended up
being stationed in Arizona and
suffered more from heat than from
Mexican desperados, the mobilization served as a rehearsal for what
would shortly occur.

Approximately 60,000 Con-
necticut inhabitants or "Nutmeggers" served in the U.S. Army
during World War I, which our
nation entered in April 1917. No
longer were there separate Connecticut regiments, but the Army
integrated men from different
states into fighting units. Racial
segregation, however, still existed
in the military and would do so
until changed by President Harry
S. Truman in the Korean War. The
state again served as an arsenal
and manufactured large amounts
of weapons and munitions. For
instance, Remington Arms in
Bridgeport produced half of the
Army's small cartridges. In
Putnam and other mill towns of
the northeastern region, mills
worked to capacity during the
war; wages, reflecting increased
output, reached their highest level
to that point; women filled many
of the newly created positions.
Patriotism ran as high as the
American flags, which increasingly flew throughout the town.
Employers sold Liberty War
Bonds on an installment basis; a
Central War Works Committee
taught new methods of canning;
the Red Cross packed and sent
supplies and surgical bandages;
residents were urged to conserve
fuel and "lightless nights" were
designated. Community life
became preoccupied with the
war effort.

Occasionally, the wartime
patriotism took on an ugly side. In

Rockville, while the German-American population did not suffer the intense anti-German feeling present in other areas of the nation, it did become increasingly self-conscious during the war, which perpetuated "Americanization." Many families had relatives fighting on both sides and an ambivalence about the war pervaded. Occasionally, in the schools, squabbles erupted with the war being fought out in the schoolyard between youths from competing ethnic groups. One German-American remembered, "it got to the point where for a few days or a week I couldn't get in at noontime because these kids would throw croquet balls at me as I came by the fence . . . ." As in other communities, the use of the German language in public was discouraged during wartime since it marked one as a potential enemy. Few wanted to be so designated. All greeted the November 11, 1918 Armistice with relief.

The distinction Americans made between Germans and their Nazi government during World War II seemed to be clearer than the difference they perceived between the German people and their government in World War I. The mobilization of the nation and the community proceeded along similar lines. In both eras, the power and authority of the federal government expanded. The raising of troops, rationing, the development of the military-industrial complex, the mobilization of the economy, the need to pay for the war, demographic shifts related to labor needs, changes affecting gender and race, all played a role in the transformation. More than 210,000 Nutmeggers fought. By the war's end in 1945, Connecticut firms had won $8 billion in war contracts, half the amount being for aircraft production. To this day, the state economy is closely connected to defense spending.

In Northeast Connecticut, World War II pervaded all facets of civilian life. In Columbia, six females organized the COGS—the Columbia Older Girls Society. From March 1943 through December 1945, they mailed their newsletter, The Cogwheel, to all servicemen at home and abroad. They raised money from weekly dances and presented an Honor Roll and flag to the town; for three years, they sent Christmas gifts to the soldiers. After the war, they honored all returning Columbian

Hector W. Storrs was one of 155 men from Mansfield who served in the Civil War. He was a private in the Twenty-second Infantry of Company E, from September 1862 until July 1863, when he was mustered out, probably after being wounded. Courtesy of Mansfield Historical Society

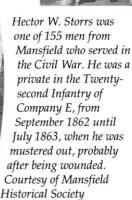

Company L, First Regiment, Connecticut National Guard, also known as the Willimantic Company, march through South Coventry in 1906. Their bedrolls indicate they are on some kind of field march or maneuver, rather than a parade. Courtesy of Lucy B. Crosbie and the Willimantic Chronicle

with a "Welcome Home" banquet. Other townswomen, as they had during the First World War, became active in the Red Cross during World War II, knitting for servicemen and making surgical dressings. Further north and east in Danielson, the National Youth Administration established a training center to prepare future "Rosie the Riveters" to work in defense-related industries. Belding Heminway in Putnam, which manufactured silk and nylon thread used in parachutes and knapsacks among other military equipment, in 1945 employed both men and women in three shifts. At the University of Connecticut in Storrs, members of the Women's Land Army, a program to ease the farm labor shortage, worked for the war effort, which obviously transcended a single gender.

While some dissent existed during World War II, it generally has been described as "The Good War" and had wide ranging support. It was a time of absolutes when an evil and dangerous enemy could be clearly defined. This still seemed to be the case in 1950 when the Korean War, in which about 70,000 Connecticut residents served, broke out. However, even then the clarity began to blur. By the time of the Vietnam War during the 1960s and early 1970s, such blurring intensified. Over 110,000 Nutmeggers served in that conflict, but the homefront was divided. Anti-war demonstrations in Storrs brought police to the UConn campus, disrupted campus recruiting, and led to a general strike after the Kent State killings in 1970. The campus,

located in the center of Northeast Connecticut, had supported the First World War and had taken on the appearance of a military camp during the Second. Like so many other colleges and universities during the Vietnam War, it reflected the divisions of our society and the rending of community in those years.

While recent times have seen the healing of these wounds, it is clear that the impact of war is significant for the sense of community. From it comes unity and cohesion or disunity and dissent. The Reverend Samuel Peters took flight to England as the result of the Revolution. In our own times, most residents chose to love Northeast Connecticut rather than leave it. With the outbreak of the Persian Gulf War in 1991, the sense of community was again being tested.

Families and friends say goodbye at the Willimantic Railroad Station (footbridge in background) as Company L, First Regiment, Connecticut National Guard leaves for the Mexican border on June 24, 1916. Stationed at Nogales, Arizona, from July to October, the troops found the burning heat more formidable than Pancho Villa. The mobilization would serve as a rehearsal for the grimmer work that lay ahead in Europe when Willimantic boys were called to service in World War I in April 1917.
Courtesy of Lucy B. Crosbie and the Willimantic Chronicle

Sheep grazing peacefully on the hill at Connecticut Agricultural College in 1917 were replacements for the grounds crew, most of whom were drafted or in the Students Army Training Corps. Coeds who lived in Grove Cottage (left) took over the male-dominated activities. In the fall they picked the apple crop and in the spring they tapped the maple trees that lined the bottom of the hill next to Route 195.
Courtesy of Historical Manuscripts and Archives, University of Connecticut Library

Members of the Rockville Red Cross chapter prepared Comfort Kits containing toilet articles for World War I recruits. Other civic and religious organizations packed and shipped boxes containing bandages, surgical dressings, hospital linen, hand-knit socks and other items. Women also learned to can and preserve food as part of the war effort.
Courtesy of Vernon Historical Society

At the end of World War I, Rockville's Mayor John Cameron welcomed home a soldier and a sailor, representing the local men who served in the war. The following year, in honor of the nineteen soldiers and sailors from the town who died in the conflict, nineteen Ginko trees were planted as a living memorial on the Maple Street School grounds.
Courtesy of Vernon Historical Society

The signing of the Armistice on November 11, 1918, was the occasion for the largest bonfire ever held at the Connecticut Agricultural College. A large crowd of army men, faculty, coeds and area residents attended the event, at which skits were performed, the Kaiser was burned in effigy, and "Joan d'Arc," wearing a white gown, rode in on a white horse. Earlier in the d classes were suspended, and snake dances and parades took plac all over the campus, in celebration of the end of the Great War.
Courtesy of Historical Manuscripts and Archives, University o Connecticut Library

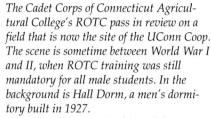

The Cadet Corps of Connecticut Agricultural College's ROTC pass in review on a field that is now the site of the UConn Coop. The scene is sometime between World War I and II, when ROTC training was still mandatory for all male students. In the background is Hall Dorm, a men's dormitory built in 1927.
Courtesy of Lucy B. Crosbie and the Willimantic Chronicle

The University of Connecticut took on the look of a military camp in 1943 when a thousand soldiers in the Army Specialized Training Program, shown here marching to their first meal, were stationed on campus for intensive engineering courses. The soldiers occupied the dorms left empty by male students who enlisted or were drafted into the service. Elsewhere on campus were other signs of war. Air-raid shelter instructions were posted on buildings; aircraft spotters maintained a 24-hour watch for enemy planes from the top of Beach Hall; and blackouts, signalled by loud blasts on the power plant whistle, interrupted evening study hours.
Courtesy of Historical Manuscripts and Archives, University of Connecticut Library

Eleanor Roosevelt looks for blisters on the hands of a farm worker in the Connecticut Women's Land Army, a program that helped ease the farm labor shortage during World War II. Mrs. Roosevelt, wife of President Franklin Roosevelt, visited the University of Connecticut in 1943 to pay tribute to the women in the program. She also met with students, inspiring one to write: "This morning Mrs. Roosevelt spoke to us at the library. It was most impressive and she was all I expected he to be—gracious, interesting and awfully well poised. She gave a message to youth."
Courtesy of Historical Manuscripts and Archives, University of Connecticut Library

A worker in the Connecticut Women's Land Army is learning to milk cows the scientific way at the University of Connecticut's College of Agriculture. She and other members of the Women's Land Army, who worked at the University farm during World War II, lived on campus and observed the same rules and curfews the women students did.
Courtesy of Historical Manuscripts and Archives, University of Connecticut Library

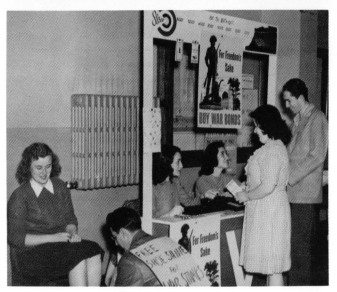

War bonds were sold in post offices, movie theatres, and even, as here, during intermission at the University of Connecticut/Yale basketball game in 1944. The UConn Student Senate sponsored the drive, and their free shoeshine offer was typical of incentives offered by many other establishments. The Bradley Theatre in Putnam, for instance, gave free admission to anyone who purchased war bonds there.
Courtesy of Historical Manuscripts and Archives, University of Connecticut Library

During World War II, workers at Wauregan Mills in Plainfield attended an awards ceremony at which the company was presented with five Navy-Army "E" awards. "E" stood for excellence, and eve worker received an "E" button, as well. The mills, which normally made cloth for commercial use, was producing fabric for the Marine Corps as part of the war effort.
Courtesy of Historical Manuscripts and Archives, University of Connecticut Library

Stafford businessmen and Boy Scouts worked together to collect scrap metal for defense plants during World War II. One of their biggest items was the old steam fire engine in the background, donated by the local fire department. As part of the war effort, residents recycled just about everything, from aluminum foil and newspapers, to used cooking fat.
Courtesy of Stafford Historical Society

In 1943, the small community of Jewish farmers in Hebron and Columbia, all members of the Columbia Synagogue, donated a fully-equipped ambulance to the United States Army. Standing in front of the ambulance on the Columbia town green are, from left to right, Sid Feldman, Shirley Barkin, Carl Frankel, Archie Berkowitz, Sam Epstein, Henry Goldman, Joe Tashlik, Max Frankel, Sol Eisenberg, Hy Sherman, and Ben Miller.
Courtesy of Irving Tannenbaum

nti-war demonstrations by Universtiy of Connecticut students
rotesting the Vietnam War sometimes created confrontations with
ie police. In 1968, three busloads of helmeted, nightstick-carrying
ate police were brought onto campus after a hundred demonstrators
isrupted job recruitment interviews by companies who manufac-
ired chemicals for the war. About a dozen protestors were arrested.
ourtesy of Historical Manuscripts and Archives, University of
onnecticut Library

In 1970, 150 students, many SDS (Students for a Democratic
Society) members, occupied the administration building at the
University of Connecticut as a protest against the Vietnam War. Ten
days later, after the Kent State killings, the protests intensified into a
general student strike and a takeover of the ROTC building by three
thousand students.
Courtesy of Historical Manuscripts and Archives, University of
Connecticut Library

Demonstrations against the Vietnam
War at the University of Connecti-
cut took many forms, from noisy
rallies and building takeovers to
candlelight vigils at Mirror Lake.
This somber scene in 1972 at the
University of Connecticut's Student
Union Mall makes an anti-war
statement without words. Courtesy
of Historical Manuscripts and
Archives, University of Connecticut
Library

Politicians always made public appearances at agricultural fairs in Northeast Connecticut. In the days before television, a country fair offered the largest possible audience in a rural area, and the fair's September and October dates were perfect timing for pre-election campaigning. In this 1940 photo at the Stafford Fair, Lt. Gov. James L. McConaughy was speaking for Gov. Raymond Baldwin, who couldn't attend because of illness. The Stafford Fair set aside one day of its week-long festivities as Governor's Day. *Courtesy of Stafford Historical Society*

Chapter Ten
PEOPLE & POLITICS

The preceding chapters have celebrated the people and places of Northeast Connecticut. This chapter concludes our family album of the northeast region. In it, we bring together photographs of the area's residents in diverse activities. However, from the quilters in Union celebrating the nation's Bicentennial to the members of Knowlton's Rangers and the Nathan Hale Fife and Drum Corps, whose photograph ends this book, the people of Northeast Connecticut share a common sense of place. From the children pictured within to the men and women who toiled in the region's shops and factories, from those who provided its police and fire protection to those like Queenie Smith, who suffered its mysteries, from the members of Windham's Venerable Club and Columbia's West Street Social Eight to the solitary "Duckman of Storrs" captured by photographer Harold Hanka, their lives, collectively and individually, shaped the fabric of Connecticut's northeast corner. It is the story of the weaving of that fabric that this volume attempts to visually portray.

Any such portrait cannot exclude the role that politics plays in shaping the character of the area. The New England political tradition is rich and continually vigorous. As early as 1672, Connecticut towns were authorized

"to choose a convenient number not exceeding seven of their inhabitants, able, discreet, and of good conversation, to be selectmen or townsmen, to take care and order the prudential affairs of the town." After Independence and with the state Constitution of 1818, each town had to annually elect selectmen; later statutes strengthened or modified such provisions. As a consequence, local government and politics has a special vitality in the Nutmeg State. In the northeast corner, this is no less the case. Town government endures and budget battles continue with as much force at the conclusion of the twentieth century as they had at the termination of the nineteenth.

Local politics often turns on issues of taxation or the most appropriate approach to education. For those who attend town meetings or sessions of their local Board of Education, it should come as no surprise that the issues they consider today rang loud years ago. National as well as local politicians gave them attention. For instance, in 1915, five thousand people gathered at Willimantic's Recreation Park heard former President William Howard Taft tell them, "One of our troubles is that we have been too lax with our youth. We do not work them hard enough. I mean in the matter of education. We give them too much vacation, not

enough training and discipline. The present generation lacks respect for authority. Many a boy thinks he knows more than his mother and father." Such an issue cut to the quick and received attention from, or reiteration by, many a School Board member. At the local level, however, matters equally basic and seemingly prosaic such as street paving, sewers, and snow plowing are fodder for politicians.

In the phrase of the former Speaker of the U.S. House of Representatives, Thomas P. "Tip" O'Neill, Jr., "All politics is local." Some politicians stayed deeply rooted in their communities. Oscar Tanner, for example, like other politicos throughout the nation's cities and towns, owned a cafe and served two terms as Willimantic's mayor. As a saloon keeper or cafe proprietor one could keep a political ear close to the ground and frequently "press the flesh" of potential voters. Such a location often served as a central gathering place and permitted easy access for political organization.

Some politicos moved beyond the region's boundaries. Several local politicians who had their beginnings in Northeast Connecticut went on to higher state office. Aside from the many who served the state in other positions, three of Connecticut's governors since colonial times listed their town of residence as one within Tolland or

Standing in front of one's home, whether an elaborate Victorian or a simple farmhouse, was a typical nineteenth-century pose. In fact, photographers traveled all across Northeast Connecticut in the late nineteenth century taking pictures of homes and families. Although their purpose was strictly commercial—selling the pictures to the homeowners—the photographs now provide documentation of the architecture of the area. The only picture here that has been positively identified is of the Burt Walker farm in Staffordville, showing the family with its horse, dog, and bicycle. Pets were considered an important part of the family and many photographs show dogs sitting in a chair or carriage. The other photographs may be in Brooklyn, Somers, or Ellington. The three people who seem to be posing in their back, rather than front, yard (with the man on the horse and the dog in the chair), may be showing off their newly acquired electricity pole.

171

Windham County. John S. Peters, a National Republican, who served from 1831 through 1833, came from Hebron; Chauncey F. Cleveland, Democrat governor from 1842 through 1844, called Hampton home; in the twentieth century, Democratic John Dempsey of Putnam held office from 1961 through 1971. A fourth governor, Wilbur Cross, who led Connecticut during the 1930s, listed his residence as New Haven. However, the Yale scholar and successful politician, had been born in the Gurleyville section of Mansfield and maintained his small town folksiness when he campaigned and governed.

At one point in the state's history, Connecticut's capital came to the northeast corner. Chauncey Cleveland, at the time of his inauguration had a broken leg and was sworn in at his home. For the occasion, the legislature passed a special act making Hampton state capital for a day. An abolitionist and temperance activist, Cleveland promoted free education, opposed imprisonment for debt, and attacked long working hours for children. Through his efforts, laws were enacted to prevent children under fourteen working more than ten hours a day—an advance for the time. Conditions in Northeast Connecticut influenced such legislation. It is likely that Cleveland was prompted in this direction by the misfortune of a young Danielson boy, who at the age of ten, lost use of his right hand in a town cotton mill accident. Local events affected state law.

More than a century later, John Dempsey ascended to the state house after making his mark as mayor of Putnam, who led the city against the ravaging floods of 1955. An Irish immigrant, he came to his adopted city three decades before the floods and was elected to Putnam's Common Council at age twenty-one during the middle of the Depression. Dempsey first went to Hartford as the town's state representative. In 1958, he was elected lieutenant governor and took the top office three years later when Abraham Ribicoff resigned to join the Kennedy administration in Washington. As governor, Dempsey supported a variety of social programs and encouraged the growth and development of the University of Connecticut during the 1960s. Despite the holding of high state office, his political roots remained firmly planted in the northeast region.

The names mentioned above are all male despite the fact that one of the major changes in recent politics has been increased participation and officeholding by women. Connecticut elected its first female governor, Ella Grasso of Windsor Locks, in 1974, but the idea of women voting, no less holding office, did not win easy acceptance. Throughout the nineteenth century and until the passage of the Nineteenth Amendment to the U.S. Constitution in 1920, the battle over suffrage raged. Its length should not be attributed to the reason offered by one Putnam resident in 1887, who remarked, "Woman suffrage . . . makes slow headway, and for the very good reason that the women of America do not want to be burdened with such a privilege."

Actually, two women from that town served as leaders in the state's suffrage movement. Dorothy Bartlett was a member of the Connecticut Woman Suffrage Association (CWSA) and the state's branch of the National Woman's Party (CNWP). She was jailed during the party's demonstrations in 1917. After the granting of suffrage in 1920, she testified at hearings on a variety of issues at the General Assembly and was defeated as a Democratic candidate for state legislature in 1924. Rosamond Danielson, also from Putnam, chaired Windham County's CWSA chapter and sat on the organization's state executive board. Once suffrage was achieved and the CWSA transformed into the Connecticut League of Women Voters since its new mission was to politically educate women who had the right to vote, Danielson stayed active in that organization. In the west of the region, Fannie Dixon Welch of Tolland, chaired the Tolland County CWSA. In 1920, immediately upon the gaining of national suffrage, she lost her election as a Democrat to become the secretary of state. However, Welch went on to become vice chair of the Democratic State Central Committee and a national committeewoman.

Such suffragists did not have an easy time obtaining their rights. Along the way they learned a great deal about political tactics, strategy, and organization. For instance, in 1893 the Connecticut legislature passed an act permitting women to vote in school board elections. Two years later, members of Willimantic's equal rights club organized a campaign to unseat a school board member and to consolidate school districts. According to Carole Nichols, "Women turned out to vote in such large numbers that the men reportedly put up a ladder to the voting hall and scrambled in ahead of the women using the stairway. The voter turnout by women increased almost 500 percent (from approximately 200 to 975 voters), and the women ere victorious." In the same city during the final years of the battle or national suffrage, Florence edyard Cross Kitchelt, the CWSA rganizer, obtained support from everal churches and the local hapter of the Odd Fellows. Her rganizing plans included distribution of literature at the town's extile mills.

Much work and effort, then, vent into the suffrage campaign nd the winning of the right for he "segregated" ballot box held y Coventry's F. Pauline Little in he photograph herein. Ironically, ome historians suggest that the

suffragists' success in achieving the right to vote set back the women's movement since all its eggs were placed in one basket.

It is argued that satisfaction with obtaining the vote dulled the fight for further female self-determination and equality between the sexes. That would come with the movement for women's liberation during and after the 1960s. By then, cultural politics complemented more traditional politics in Northeast Connecticut and in the nation.

Nevertheless, the region's people and politics continued in

old ways as well. Pattern and predictability vie with the episodic and novelty in the northeast corner to keep matters always interesting, invigorating and inspiring. Residents of the region, while divided into twenty-eight separate towns, share a common character imprinted by its mills and meadows. As we close this volume, we recognize the area's diversity as well as its common identity and hope that we have done justice to both.

ourtesy of Marion Emmons

Attitudes toward children at the turn of the century were varied, ranging from sternness to indulgence. The older generation still considered obedience to be a prime virtue, as evidenced in the photograph of William H. Gardiner with his grandchildren, nieces and nephews at his Mansfield home (shown on the preceding page). However, parents increasingly saw children as having special needs and interests of their own. Certainly the wide range of clothing and expressions of the five Vernon children attest to their individuality. Special furniture for children was a new concept, like the fancy perambulator in the portrait of the Colburn children of Stafford. Photographs themselves became less formal and more candid, capturing a charming moment, as the Putnam child holding her cat next to the phonograph. As sentimentalism toward children became more pervasive, childhood turned into a cult. Sweet, innocent children were an ideal, however, sometimes achieved in photographs, but rarely in reality.

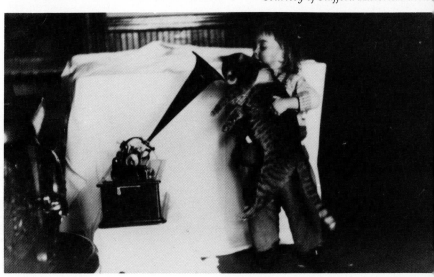

May 1 was Hospital Day at Stafford's Johnson Memorial Hospital for many years. Mothers brought their babies, as well as older children, who danced around the maypole on the hospital lawn while the younger ones watched. The photograph is dated 1925, thirteen years after the hospital opened. The first baby delivered here was Edith Ruby Limburger, who later returned, not just for a Hospital Day reunion, but as a nurse, eventually becoming assistant superintendent in the 1940s. This small-town hospital was self-sufficient for many years, raising its own chickens and cows, fruits and vegetables.
Courtesy of Stafford Historical Society

While the majority of women workers were employed in the large mills or on the farms or in offices, many worked in small shops or businesses such as this millinery company, possibly in Ellington. Presumably the three women in aprons are the hatmakers modeling their creations, and the woman to the left is either the owner or a customer. While women often made their own clothes, they left millinery to specialists. General store styles were too general for the fashion-minded woman, who either shopped for one-of-a-kind hats at local milliners, or for high-style ones through catalogues.
Courtesy of State Archives, Connecticut State Library

Adeline Gelinas Brennan, a secretary in a Willimantic law office, posed for this picture in 1911, with the tools of her trade, the telephone and typewriter. The invention of the typewriter and the telephone proved to be two milestones in the employment of women.
Courtesy of Lucy B. Crosbie and the Willimantic Chronicle

Queenie Smith, of Stafford, was dubbed a "backwoods Cleopatra" in a tabloid-style newspaper account of her disappearance and suspected murder in 1919. At the time, Queenie had been married three times. When a female skull was discovered on a Stafford farm fourteen years later, it was thought to be that of Queenie. A Stafford farmer was implicated but never convicted because of lack of sufficient evidence. When the farmer died a short time later, Queenie appeared at his funeral, attended by her fourth husband, and eventually went on to marry again.
Courtesy of Laura Knott Twine

Time stands still as these workmen stop to pose for photographer Julian Beville who took a series of mill and village pictures in Willimantic just after the turn of the twentieth century.
Courtesy of Lucy B. Crosbie and the Willimantic Chronicle

Even after the organization of work had changed so that large numbers of people toiled together in one place called a factory, some individual craftsmen remained to ply their trades alone or in small groups. Here, Erose Belanger repairs shoes in his shop in Stafford. In the service society of today's post-industrial America, the number of self-employed skilled craftsmen has diminished greatly.
Courtesy of Stafford Historical Society

o Heinige of Storrs, was a familiar figure to ducks and humans alike at Mirror Lake on the niversity of Connecticut campus. His twice-daily feeding of these feathered residents sparked controversy between groups that supported his efforts and those that opposed them.
arold Hanka photograph; courtesy of the photographer

A dozen of Willimantic's finest, comprising the city's entire police force, pose at the entrance to the police station in the Town Hall building in 1900. Front left is the Chief, Captain F. H. Richmond; front right is Lieutenant, later Captain, Daniel Killourey. The fourth man in the second row, Thomas Grady, would also become chief of police. The second officer from the left in the back row is Louis Paulhus. Other patrolmen pictured are John J. Manley, Charles L. Anderson, Edward Kennedy, Charles W. Snow, W. J. Hastings, John J. Keirans, C. V. Enander, and Judson A. Potter. When the city municipal offices moved into the new Windham Town Hall building in 1897, the then Chief of Police William Hillhouse proclaimed the quarters the finest to house any police department in Connecticut.
Courtesy of Lucy B. Crosbie and the Willimantic Chronicle

Standing tall and looking proud, members of the fledgling North Windham Fire Department, founded in 1926, pose with their new truck in 1931. The Windham Center Volunteer Fire Department dates back to 1824, and the South Windham Department was organized in 1911. In the three villages of Windham, outside of Willimantic, membership in the volunteer fire department continues to be a matter of great pride. In years past, much of a community's social life centered around the local volunteer fire department.
Courtesy of Lucy B. Crosbie and the Willimantic Chronicle

These five Stafford Masons, of Wolcott
Lodge No. 60, circa 1900, could enjoy their
lodge membership without having to endure
the anti-Masonic sentiment that was
prevalent throughout the United States less
than a hundred years earlier. In some
Northeast Connecticut communities, such
as Woodstock, Masons could not be elected
to town office and were not allowed to
become church members. By the late
nineteenth century, however, the feeling
against secret orders had died away, and
there were two Masonic Lodges in Stafford.
Courtesy of Stafford Historical Society

"Yea, if a man live a great many years, let
him rejoice in them all." Hotelman Seth
Hooker called to order the first meeting of the
Venerable Club, for men 70 years and older,
shown assembled on the veranda of the
Hooker House. The aggregate age of those
pictured was 3,841 years, the average age,
77. The oldest was Marvin Lincoln, 87, born
in 1813, and his younger brothers Loren, 83,
and Orrin, 77, were with him.
*Courtesy of Lucy B. Crosbie and the
Willimantic Chronicle*

The West Street Social Eight was a women's
club in Columbia whose purpose was to
sponsor neighborhood projects as well as
social events. They raised money for their
projects by making quilts and putting on
plays, oyster suppers, and card parties. One
of their first projects was to purchase iron
gates for the West Street Cemetery. The
seven members pictured in the photo, circa
1905, are (standing) Mrs. DuToit, Candice
Buell, Carrie Utley, Ella Hutchinson, and
(seated) Emily Cobb, Jennie Isham, and
Mrs. Friedrich.
Courtesy of Columbia Historical Society

These dapper Willimantic gentlemen are on their best behavior as they pose for this outing portrait identified only as "July 12, 1888 - Before." Perhaps they are assembled for some political outing because the man in the rear, third from the right, seems to have a fan with a man's picture on it. Whomever they are, when we view the companion picture titled "July 12, 1888 - After," we know they had a sense of humor. The men have taken advantage of the opportunity to record a bit of self-mockery for the photographer. That each of them entered into the fun indicates they had a good time at the outing they so carefully recorded for posterity. When we look at the picture now, we smile, as they knew we would when they posed for us on that sunny afternoon more than a hundred years ago. *Courtesy of Lucy B. Crosbie and the* Willimantic Chronicle

Besides a home delivery service (see Chapter 4), George Woods had a meat market on Main Street in Stafford Springs. People shopped daily and had their meat cut to order on the chopping block next to the counter. The sawdust on the floor absorbed the fat from the meat. The meat market was an early convenience store, selling canned goods and barrel pickles as well.
Courtesy of Stafford Historical Society

The rather formally dressed patrons of the drugstore of Samuel Chesbro in Willimantic pose for the camera in 1896. An array of medicines and remedies are in the cases to the left, and to the right a cone-shaped display holds natural sponges for the bath. The case at the right seems to hold bottles of spirits which every well-equipped drugstore dispensed at the turn of the century. The store was illuminated by fixtures that combined gas and electricity. The ceiling of pressed tin displayed a roccoco design. Samuel Chesbro had reason to take pride in this stylish pharmacy.
Courtesy of Lucy B. Crosbie and the Willimantic Chronicle

Four barbers waited to serve you at the shop of Adelard A. Monast in the basement of the Hooker Hotel in Willimantic, circa 1910. Many men went to the barber shop daily to be shaved. Visible in the mirror is the cabinet containing brushes and mugs bearing the names of regular customers in gold letters.
Courtesy of Lucy B. Crosbie and the Willimantic Chronicle

Three bartenders were ready to serve customers at Cloutier's Tavern in Putnam, circa 1900. The bar was located at the rear of the Bugbee House in Union Square. *Courtesy of Aspinock Historical Society of Putnam*

Oscar Tanner, two-term mayor of Willimantic, whose business advertisements proclaimed that he was "a personal friend of the great prizefighter John L. Sullivan," posed in front of his cafe in 1900 with a patron, the bartender, and the deliveryman from the Thread City Bottling Works next door. The wagon is typical of vehicles used to deliver beer. The driver carried a small cushion he placed on the sidewalk. As he heaved the casks of brew from the wagon, he could usually target them perfectly to land on the cushion. *Courtesy of Lucy B. Crosbie and the Willimantic Chronicle*

Attilio Frassinelli, pictured here working with Mildred McLogan at a Stafford grocery store, rose through town politics to become lieutenant governor of Connecticut in 1967. He took office exactly one hundred years after another Stafford resident, Ephraim Hyde, was also elected lieutenant governor. John Dempsey, another Northeast Connecticut resident, was governor during Frassinelli's term. *Courtesy of Stafford Historical Society*

Although Wilbur Cross spent a distinguished career as a Yale scholar before becoming governor of Connecticut in 1930 at the age of sixty-eight, he never lost his down-to-earth manner or forgot his rural roots. Born in the miller's house across from the Gurleyville Gristmill in Mansfield, he returned to his boyhood village to campaign at a local turkey farm. His folksy style endeared him to farmers and small-town residents, who helped elect him governor for four terms during the Depression.
Courtesy of Mansfield Historical Society

John Dempsey, governor of Connecticut from 1961 to 1971, clasps the arm of Putnam Police Chief Omer Mathurin, who served under him during Dempsey's six-term tenure as mayor of Putnam. Standing next to Dempsey are his wife, Mary, and Raymond Jackson, a selectman from Pomfret. The man on the right is unidentified. Dempsey emigrated with his family from Ireland in 1915, at the age of ten, to Putnam, where his family found employment at the Putnam Woolen Company. After attending local schools, Dempsey rose quickly in town politics. As mayor he led Putnam through the devastating flood of 1955, winning statewide recognition for his efforts. Courtesy of Aspinock Historical Society of Putnam

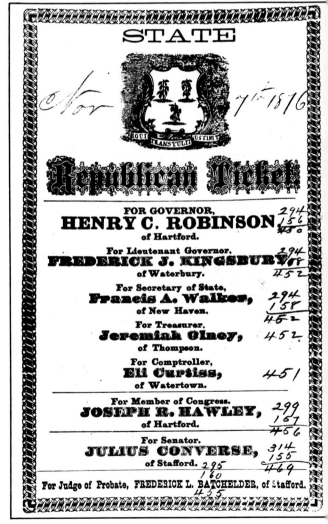

These nineteenth-century party tickets served as informal tallies after votes were counted. The Democratic Ticket shows the results of local Stafford elections. The Republican Ticket, for state elections in 1876, lists the candidates' hometowns, with a few from Northeast Connecticut. Courtesy of Stafford Historical Society

In the days before voting machines, paper ballots were put in wooden boxes and hand counted—even as they are in some towns today. William J. Rieggers (right), the newly elected second selectman of Stafford is celebrating his victory with town clerk and treasurer Harold Andrews in this 1934 photo.
Courtesy of Stafford Historical Society

F. Pauline Little of Coventry holds a reminder of the not-too-distant past when women's votes were cast in a separate ballot box. The practice began in 1920, after the constitutional amendment gave women the right to vote. In the background, Mary Walsh and Arlene Ferguson sit by an "integrated" ballot box used by 1989 voters. The issue was a referendum on the town budget.
Frances L. Funk photograph; courtesy of the photographer

Anna Mae Pallanck (second from left) was the first First Selectwoman in Union in that town's 250-year history. She served in that capacity from 1973 to 1980. Since then, Jane Harwood became the second First Selectwoman in Union in 1985. Mrs. Pallanck is presiding at a 1978 town meeting, a form of government that has remained popular in Union—the smallest town in the state—throughout its history. Also in the picture are Selectman Nathan Swift, Jr., Moderator Lloyd Eaton, and Town Clerk Patricia Kavanagh. *Courtesy of Union Historical Society*

The country's Bicentennial in 1976 sparked many town and community projects, including the making of a Bicentennial Quilt in Union by members of the Golden Age Club. The quilt, appropriately named "Union Star," was raffled off to raise money for other Bicentennial events, which included a costume ball and 1776 church service, as well as a traditional parade. The quilters are Marion Kingsbury, Anna Leighton, Mabel Bradway, and Edith Agard. *Courtesy of Union History Society*

Frank Galinat (left), commander of Knowlton's Rangers, leads his men in a cheer at a July 4, 1980 performance at the Salvation Army Camp in Coventry. Behind them is another local group, the Nathan Hale Fife and Drum Corps. The Rangers recreate Revolutionary War battles using flintlock weapons. Galinat had been a jet-engine assembler who also practiced the ancient craft of cutting flints for muskets and other eighteenth-century weapons. The region is made up of many such individuals, who live in the present and look to the future, at the same time remembering the historic past of Northeast Connecticut. *Frances L. Funk photograph; courtesy of the photographer*

BIBLIOGRAPHY

bbott, Ardis. "Rockville's Germans: A Singing Society." *Tri-Town Reporter*, Bicentennial Supplement, July 4, 1976.

shford, 1714–1989, Moments from History. Ashford [Conn.] 275th Anniversary Committee, 1990.

rber, John Warner. *Connecticut Historical Collections*. New Haven: Durrie & Peck and J. W. Barber, 1836.

rth, Gunther. *City People*. New York: Oxford University Press, 1980.

ardsley, Tom, interviewer. Interview of Rose Dunham, March 21, 1990. Willimantic, Conn.: Oral History Collection, Windham Textile and History Museum.

ardsley, Tom. Willimantic Women: Their Lives and Labors. Willimantic, Conn.: Windham Textile and History Museum, 1990.

wen, Clarence Winthrop. *The History of Woodstock, Connecticut*. Privately Published, 1926.

rke, Doreen Bolger. *J. Alden Weir, An American Impressionist*. Newark: University of Delaware Press, 1983.

ameron, Diane Maher. *Eastford, The Biography of a New England Town*. Eastford[Conn.] Historical Society, 1976.

entennial of Vernon (Rockville), 1808–1908. Souvenir Program, Rockville, Conn., 1908.

arles Ethan Porter, 1847?–1923. Marlborough: Connecticut Gallery, Inc. 1987.

ronology of Mansfield, Connecticut, 1702–1972. Mansfield Historical Society, History Workshop, 1974.

ronology of Willington, Connecticut, 1727–1927. Willington Historical Society, History Committee, 1977.

aniels, Bruce C. *The Connecticut Town, Growth and Development, 1635-1790*. Middletown, Conn.: Wesleyan University Press, 1979.

avidge, Carol K. "Northeast Album, A Photographic History of People at Work in Windham County." *The Hartford Courant Magazine*, July 26, 1981.

avis, Alison. *Hampton Remembers, A Small Town in New England, 1885–1950*. Privately Published, 1976.

emers, Ronald F. *Modernization in a New England Town, A History of Willington, Connecticut*. Willington Historical Society, 1983.

unwell, Steve. *The Run of the Mill*. Boston: David R. Godine, 1978.

rly Ellington Village and Supplement. Ellington, Conn.: Congregational Church, Calendar Staff, 1952.

cyclopedia of American History. New York: Harper & Row, 1965.

ude, Wilson and Friedland, Joan. *Connecticut Firsts*. Chester, Conn.: Globe Pequot Press, 1978.

anklin, John Hope. *From Slavery to Freedom*. 4th ed. New York: Alfred A. Knopf, 1974.

riggs, Susan J. *Folklore and Firesides in Pomfret, Hampton and Vicinity*. Pomfret, Conn., 1950.

rundberg, Andy. "Reality Reels As Photo Tricks Are Refined." *International Herald Tribune*, August 17, 1990.

anka, Harold. *Positive Images*. Willimantic, Conn.: The Chronicle Printing Co., 1982.

artford Courant, selected issues.

arwood, Pliny LeRoy. *History of Eastern Connecticut*. 2 vols. New Haven: The Pioneer Historical Publishing Co., 1932.

ill, Evan. *University of Connecticut Centennial History Appendix*. Unpublished, 1982.

hnson, Malcolm L. *Yesterday's Connecticut*. Miami, Fla.: E. A. Seemann Publishing, 1976.

ent, Louise Andrews. *Village Greens of New England*. New York: M. Barrows & Co., Inc., 1948.

arned, Ellen D. *History of Windham County, Connecticut*. 2 vols. Bicentennial Edition. Chester, Conn.: The Pequot Press, 1976.

Lincoln, Allen B., ed. 2 vols. *A Modern History of Windham County, Connecticut*. Chicago: S. J. Clarke Publishing Co., 1920.

Lussier, Janet. "Remembering the Actors' Colony." *Tolland County Times*, July 26, 1990.

Lutz, Hazel P. *Vernon Vignettes*. 2 vols. The Vernon [Conn.] Historical Society, 1970 & 1976.

Messier, Betty Brook and Aronson, Janet Sutherland. *The Roots of Coventry, Connecticut*. Coventry, 1987.

Miller, Ross. *American Apocalypse: The Great Fire and the Myth of Chicago*. Chicago: University of Chicago Press, 1990.

New York, New Haven, and Hartford Railroad Records. Storrs, Conn.: University of Connecticut Archives, 1989.

Nichols, Carole. *Votes and More for Women: Suffrage and After in Connecticut*. New York: The Institute for Research in History and The Haworth Press, Inc.,1983.

Palmer, Michele. *Decades of Pride, A History of the School of Home Economics and Family Studies, The University of Connecticut*. Storrs, Conn.: School of Home Economics & Family Studies, The University of Connecticut, 1981.

Parent, Steve. "Razed But Remembered." Term paper submitted to History of Urban America course, University of Connecticut, December 2, 1975.

"People At Work, 1880–1940." Brochure accompanying photographic exhibit. Quinebaug Valley Community College Library, 1981.

Polenberg, Richard. *War and Society*. Philadelphia: J. B. Lippincott, Co., 1972.

Rader, Benjamin. *American Sports*. Englewood Cliffs, N.J.: Prentice-Hall, 1983.

Register and Manual. Hartford: State of Connecticut, 1985.

Reiss, Steven. *City Games*. Urbana: University of Illinois, 1983.

Reps, John W. *Town Planning in Frontier America*. Trenton, N.J.: Princeton University Press, 1969.

Rifkind, Carole. *Main Street: The Face of Urban America*. New York: Harper & Row, 1977.

Rosen, Christine M. *The Limits of Power: Great Fires and the Process of City Growth in America*. Cambridge, England: Cambridge University Press, 1986.

Rosenzweig, Roy. *Eight Hours for What We Will*. Cambridge, England: Cambridge University Press, 1983.

Roth, David M., ed. *Connecticut History and Culture: An Historical Overview and Resource Guide for Teachers*. Hartford: The Connecticut Historical Commission, 1985. Of special note: Joseph W. Duffy, "Connecticut at War"; Thomas R. Lewis, "Geography"; Leslie P. Ricklin, "Education"; John Sutherland, "Immigration"; Janice L. & Jerrold B. Trecker, "Sports."

School Memories: Columbia, 1732–1948. Columbia, Conn. The Columbia Historical Society, 1976.

Series in Connecticut History, 5 volumes. Chester, Conn.: The Pequot Press, 1975.

    Vol. 1: Albert E. Van Dusen. *Puritans Against the Wilderness: Connecticut History to 1763*.

    Vol. 2: David M. Roth and Freeman Meyer. *From Revolution to Constitution: Connecticut 1763 to 1818*.

    Vol. 3: Janice Law Trecker. *Preachers, Rebels and Traders: Connecticut 1818 to 1865*.

    Vol. 4: Ruth O. M. Andersen. *From Yankee to American: Connecticut 1865 to 1914*.

    Vol. 5: Herbert F. Janick, Jr. *A Diverse People: Connecticut 1914 to the Present*.

Sibun, John. *Our Town's Heritage, 1708–1958, Hebron, Connecticut.* Douglas Library of Hebron, 1975.

Somers, Connecticut: Thru The Camera's Eye. Somers Historical Society, 1978.

Stafford Historical Highlights, 1776–1976. Stafford [Conn.] Bicentennial Commission, Heritage Committee, 1976.

Stave, Bruce M. "An Autobiography." *Hartford Courant,* June 10, 1979.

——."Introduction" to special issue on "Photography and Urban History." *Journal of Urban History* (May 1989), pp. 243–246.

——."Running Away." Unpublished manuscript.

——."Wintertime and the Living is Easy." *New York Times,* January 29, 1984.

Story of Columbia, The. Columbia, Conn.: Columbia Congregational Church, Women's Guild, 1954.

Terkel, Studs. *The Good War.* New York: Ballantine Books, 1984.

Thompson Bicentennial Memory Book, 1785-1985. Thompson, Conn.: Bicentennial Book Committee, 1985.

Turner, Gregg M. & Jacobus, Melancthon W. *Connecticut Railroads: An Illustrated History.* Hartford: Connecticut Historical Society, 1986.

Tuttle, Sam. Sam *Tuttle's Picture Book of Old Connecticut.* Scotia, N.Y.: American Review, 1979.

250th Anniversary Celebration, Tolland, Connecticut, 1715–1965. Souvenir Program, 1965.

Upson, Jeannine, ed. *Union Lands, A People's History.* The Union [Conn.] Historical Society, 1984.

Van Dusen, Albert E. *Connecticut.* New York: Random House, 1961.

Warner, Sam Bass, Jr. *The Urban Wilderness.* New York: Harper & Row, 1972.

Weaver, Margaret. *Perspectives of Putnam.* The Aspinock Historical Society of Putnam, Connecticut, 1980.

Weigold, Harold, comp. *Tolland, The History of an Old Connecticut Post Road Town.* Chester, Conn.: The Pequot Press, 1971.

Willimantic Daily Chronicle, Special Anniversary Edition, September 8 1967, and selected issues.

Zucker, Paul. *Tower and Square: From the Agora to the Village Green.* New York: Columbia University Press, 1959.

INDEX

A

Abington, 128, 142
Actors' Colony, 135, 142
Adams, John, 134, 137
Advent Society, 128
Aetna Life Insurance Company, 136
Agard, Edith, 186
Aldrich Manufacturing Company, 42
Alexander's Lake, 86
Almy, William, 36
Almyville, 54
American Legion, Stafford Springs, 66
American Mill, 37
American Thread Company, 29, 36, 37, 38, 40, 42, 43, 44,47, 48, 49, 50, 51, 52, 53, 55, 91, 118, 119, 120, 127
Amston Motor Car Company, 79
Anderson, Charles L., 178
Andover, 22,73
Andrews, Harold, 185
Army Specialized Training Program, 165
Arnold family 134
Arnold, Ansel, Mrs., 139
Arnold, Benedict, 160
Arnold, William, 139
Aronson, Janet, 115
Aronson, Ron, 115
Ashford, 12, 89, 97, 102, 136, 149, 160, 161. *See also* Warrenville
Ashford Bible Society, 129
Ashley, Alice, 92
Ashley, Edward, 92
Ashley, Helen, 92
Attawaugan, 136
Atwood, James III, 48
Atwood, James, 37, 42

B

Bacon Academy, 97
Baldwin, Raymond, 168
Ballouville, 86

Baltic, 87
Barber, John Warner, 10, 12, 59
Barkin, Shirley, 166
Barrows, Colonel, 37, 38
Bartlett, Dorothy, 172
Bartlett, George A., 140
Beach, Charles L., 111
Beck, Audrey, 105
Belanger, Erose, 177
Belding-Heminway-Corticelli Silk Company, 38, 163
Bennett, Frederick, 19
Bennett, Mildred, 19
Benton, Clarence, 21
Berkowitz, Archie, 166
Bernier, Adolph, 143
Beville, Julian, 90, 142, 176
Bissell, Irvin G., 140
Blizzard of 1888, 148, 150
Blizzard of 1978, 149, 150
Block and Bridle Show, 14
Bolton, 10, 58
Boss, General Eugene, 91
Boss, Helen, 91
Boston-Hartford Turnpike, 74
Bowen, Henry C., 134, 137
Bowen, Jessie S., 111
Bradley Theatre, 135, 139, 166
Bradway Farm, 19, 20
Bradway, Mabel, 186
Bradway, Ruth, 99
Branchville, 40
Brennan, Adeline Gelinas, 176
Brigham Tavern, 82
Brooklyn, 21, 23, 58, 98, 130, 171. *See also* East Brooklyn
Brooklyn Fair, 31
Brown, Smith, 36
Brown, Walter, 83
Brunell, Mr. & Mrs. Fred, 84
Buckley, Morgan G., 136
Budd Car, 92

Buell, Candice, 179
Bugbee House, 182

C

Calvary Baptist Church, Willimantic, 131
Cameron, John, 164
Canadian Athletic Club, 119, 123
Canterbury, 26, 61, 97, 103
Capitol Theatre, 135
Carocari, F., 126
Central Vermont Railway, 77, 88, 89, 150
Central War Works Committee, 161
Chaplin, 79, 89, 102
Chaplin Fair, 31
Charter Oaks, 136
Chase, Bill, 133
Chautauqua, 135
Chesbro, Ernest P., 83
Chesbro, Samuel, 181
Chickering House, 90
Church, Frederick, 123
City Hotel, 64
Civil War, 160, 161, 162
Clemens, Mildred, 135
Cleveland, Chauncey F., 172
Cloutier's Tavern, 182
Cobb, Emily, 179
Codfish Falls, 112
Colchester and Andover Mail Stage, 73
Columbia, 19, 58, 81, 87, 98, 102, 121, 136, 165, 166, 170, 179
Columbia Older Girls Society, 162
Congregation Agudath Achim, Columbia, 121
Congregational Church, Coventry, 62
Congregational Church, Ellington, 129
Congregational Church, Rockville, 37
Congregational Church, Scotland, 61
Congregational Church, Stafford Springs, 1..
Congregational Church, Storrs, 141
Congregational Church, Willimantic, 146
Congregational Church, Woodstock, 59, 131

onnecticut Agricultural College. *See* University of Connecticut
onnecticut Historical Commission, 103
onnecticut Infantry, Company E, Third Regiment, 159
onnecticut Jewish Farmers Association, 19
onnecticut League of Women Voters, 172
onnecticut Milk Producers Association, 20
onnecticut National Guard, Company L, First Regiment, 67, 161, 162, 163
onnecticut State College. *See* University of Connecticut
onnecticut Woman Suffrage Association (CWSA), 172, 173
onnecticut Women's Land Army, 163, 165
onsolidated Railway Company, 78
onverse, Mabel, 141
onwell, Russell, 135
oventry, 12, 58, 62, 78, 82, 87, 124, 135, 136, 141, 142, 173, 185, 186. *See also* South Coventry
oventry Lake. *See* Lake Wangumbaug
randall, Prudence, 97, 98, 103
imean War, 36
oss, Wilber, 172, 183
urtis, Don H., 38

D

anielson, 24, 38, 53, 76, 86, 87, 105, 136, 163, 172
anielson, Rosamond, 172
avis, Jimmy, 22
Leo, Gertrude, 105
empsey, John, 149, 53, 172, 182, 184
empsey, Mary, 184
evereaux, Art, 81
oubleday, General Abner, 136
ockman of Storrs. *See* Heinige, Leo
agan Mill, 55
maine, "Buck", Jr., 92
unham Hall Building, 55
unham Hall Library, 37, 49
unham, Austin, 36
unn, Daniel P., 66, 140
unn, Mayor Daniel P., 161
Toit, Mrs., 179

E

O. Smith High School, 81
gle Manufacturing Company, 161
gleville, 77, 80, 88, 144, 161
st Brooklyn, 51
st Thompson, 89, 150
st Windsor, 21
stbrook Mall, 71
stern Connecticut State College. *See* Eastern Connecticut State University
stern Connecticut State University, 65, 99, 107, 108, 109, 110, 136
stern States Express, 150
shford, 25, 89, 98, 141. *See also* North Ashford, Phoenixville
shford Bicycle Club, 141
shford House, 141
ton, Lloyd, 186
enezer Lutheran Church, Willimantic, 130
mondston, Arlene, 105
enberg, Sol, 166
s Fairgrounds, 29
ington, 19, 21, 171, 175

Elms Boarding House, 50
Elms, The, 119
Enander, C. V., 178
Enfield, 21
Epstein, Sam, 166
European House Hotel, 64

F

Feldman, Sid, 166
Fenton, Harriet Bass, 154
Ferguson, Arlene, 185
First Baptist Church, Willimantic, 130
Flint, George W., 111
Footbridge, Willimantic, 62, 64
Four Town Fair, 21
Frankel, Carl, 166
Frankel, Max, 166
Franklin Automobile Agency, 83
Frassinelli, Attilio, 182
French & Indian War, 160
French River, 149
Friedrich, Mrs., 179
Fuller's Tavern, 82

G

Galinat, Frank, 186
Gardiner, William H., 173, 174
Garrigus, H. L., 14
Garrison, William Lloyd, 98
Gejdensen, Sam, 105
Gem Theatre, 135
General Lyon Inn, 141
George, Tate, 145
Gilead, 136
Girard Park, 142
Glaude, Aimee, 106
Golden Age Club, Union, 186
Golden Agers, Stafford, 89
Goldman, Henry, 166
Goodman, Col. Richard J., 67
Goodwin, Dorothy, 105
Gormley, Claire, 99
Grady, Thomas, 178
Graff, George, 99
Grant Company, W. T., 69
Grant, Ulysses S., 137
Grasso, Ella, 172
Graves, Washington, 66
Great Wall of Sterling, 27
Grosvenor Dale Mills, 34
Grovsvenor Dale Company Fire Department, 81
Guardello, Joey, 104
Gurleyville, 74, 172, 183
Gurleyville Gristmill, 183

H

H. P. Hood and Company, 18
Hale, Nathan, 58
Hampton, 23, 89, 102, 148, 172
Hanson, Tony, 145
Harbeck's Cash Store, 24
Harrison, William Henry, 137
Hartford, 136
Hartford and Willimantic Jitney Association, 87
Hartford Convention, 160
Hartford, Manchester & Rockville Tramway Company, 78
Harwood, Jane, 186
Hastings, W. J., 178

Hayden, Mrs. James E., 65
Hayden, Whiting, 65
Hayes, Rutherford B., 137
Hebron, 19, 59, 73, 79, 87, 102, 121, 136, 148, 160, 166, 172. *See also* Gilead, Turnerville
Hebron Fair, 31
Heinige, Leo, 170, 177
Henken, D. H., 64
Hevey Farm, 23
Hickey, Eugene, 77
Hillhouse, William, 178
Hinman, George E., 140
Hirsch, Baron Maurice de, 19
Hockanum River, 37
Holt, Constance, 137
Hooker Hotel, 179, 181
Hooker, Reverend Thomas, 74
Hooker, Seth, 179
Horsebarn Hill, 33
Horseshoe Park, 29
Horsman, Reverend Ruth, 99
Howard, Ellis, 152
Hurley, James, 140
Hurricane Diane, 152, 153
Hurricane of 1938, 146, 147, 148, 149, 151, 156, 157
Hutchins, William, 42
Hutchinson, Ella, 179
Hyde, Ephraim, 182

I

Institute for Physical Education, 104
Isham, Jennie, 179

J

Jackson, Raymond, 184
Jacobs, Helene, 107
Jaworsky, Nadja, 127
Jefferson, Thomas, 18
Jewish Agricultural Society, 19
Jewish Colonization Association, 19
Jillson family, 36
Jillson House, 70, 71, 126
Jillson Square, 65, 66, 67, 154
Jillson, William, 70, 76
Johnson, Charlie, 141
Johnson Memorial Hospital, 175
Johnston, Kevin, 105
Jones, James, 77
Jones, Reverend David, 129
Jordan Hardware Company Fire, 154
Jordan, C. H., 77
Jorday, William P., 140
Joy, M. R., 78

K

Kavanagh, Patricia, 186
Keigwin, Lewis L., 140
Keirans, John J., 178
Keith, Dana, 141
Keith, Mary, 141
Kennedy, Edward, 178
Kent State, 163, 167
Kent, Elder, 128
Killingly, 86. *See also* Attawaugan, Ballouville, Danielson, Dayville
Killourey, Daniel, 178
Kingsbury, Marion, 186
Kirby Mill, 55
Kitchelt, Florence Ledyard Cross, 173

Kneeland, Josephine, 107
Knowlton's Rangers, 136, 170, 186
Knowlton, Thomas, 12, 160
Koons, Benjamin, 111
Korean War, 161, 163
Kramer Middle School, 102
Kratochvil, Joseph, 99
Krug, Abraham, 126

L

Ladies of the Universalist Church, 26
Lake Wangumbaug, 135, 141, 142
Lakin, Lora Whitney, 108
LaPierre, Dr. Julian, 136
Larned, Ellen, 138
Lebanon, 77,136
Leed's Mill, 37
Leighton, Anna, 186
Lexington, Battle of, 58
Liberty Bell, 92
Liberty War Bonds, 161
Liedertafel, 136
Life Magazine, 146
Limburger, Edith Ruby, 175
Limited Express. See New England Limited
Lincoln Furniture Store, 65
Lincoln Square. See Jillson Square
Lincoln, Loren, 179
Lincoln, Marvin, 179
Lincoln, Orrin, 179
Little, F. Pauline, 173, 185
Little, Fred, 83
Little, Harriette May, 108
Loeser, Mabel, 135
Loeser, William, 135
Lombardo, Frank P., 126
Loomer Opera House, 69, 135, 139

M

Maine, U.S.S., 159, 161
Malbone, Godfrey, 130
Malone, James F., 92
Manchester, 36
Manhasset Company, 41
Manley, John J., 178
Mansfield, 55, 74, 77, 81, 82,98, 102, 142, 150, 161, 162, 172, 173, 174, 183.*See also*
    Eagleville, Gurleyville, Mansfield
    Depot, Mansfield, Hollow, Merrow,
    Storrs
Mansfield Depot, 77, 88
Mansfield Hollow, 55
Mansfield Training School, 99, 104, 105
Mashamoquet Brook State Park, 142
Masons, 179
Mateo, Luisa, 127
Mathurin, Omer, 184
May Festival, 129
McCabe, E. J., 92
McConaughy, James L., 168
McDonald, John, 146
McKinley, William, 81, 137, 161
McLogan, Mildred, 182
Merrow, 77, 88
Mexican War, 160
Meyer, Christine, 92
Middle River, 149
Miller, Ben, 166
Miller, Robert E., 105
Mohegan Indians, 74
Molinaro, Louis, 116

Molinaro, Samuel, 116
Molinaro, Vincent, 116
Monast, Adelard A., 181
Moor's Indian Charity School, 102
Moosup, 42, 137
Moriarty, J. Francis, 92
Morreale, Salvatore, 105
Moxon, David, 42
Muraco, Carmine, 116
Murdoch's Farm, 22
Murray, H. C., 67

N

Nash, George W., 45
Natchaug River, 142
Natchaug School, 95
Nathan Hale Fife and Drum Corps, 170, 186
Nathan Hale Homestead, 12, 141
Nathan Hale Hotel, 64, 65
National Thread Company, 55
National Woman's Party, 172
National Youth Administration, 163
New England Home Photo Company, 60
New England Limited, 89, 148
New England Transportation Company, 88
New Haven Railroad, 88
New London, Willimantic & Springfield Rail-
    road, 76
New Village, 50
New York, New Haven and Hartford Rail-
    road, 90, 92
Newton, Charles B., 140
Nichols, Leslie, 83
Noble School, 101, 107
North Ashford, 98
North Grosvenordale, 76, 82, 93, 122
North Windham, 149
North Windham Fire Department, 178
Norwich and Worcester Railroad, 76
Notre Dame de Bon Secours Elementary
    School, 101

O

O'Neil, Reverend Felix, 66
O'Neill, Thomas P. "Tip," 170
O'Neill, William, 105
Old School and Home Week Parade, 67
Old State House, 160
Old Trinity Church, Brooklyn, 130
Oliver, Frank, 151
Olson, George, 99
Oneco, 25, 27

P

Pallanck, Anna Mae, 186
Partrick, Sara, 107
Paulhus, Louis, 178
Pawtucket, Rhode Island, 36
People's Tramway Company, 78, 86
Pequot War, 160
Peters, John S., 172
Peters, Reverend Samuel, 160, 163
Phoenixville, 19
Pierce, Earle, 133
Pinney, E. C., 26
Plainfield, 20, 82, 92, 124, 149, 152, 166. *See
    also* Almyville, Moosup, Wauregan
Polish-American Club, 121, 123
Pomfret, 17, 21, 22, 85, 87, 89, 96, 103, 128,
    142, 160, 184. *See also* Abington, Pomfret
    Landing

Pomfret Landing, 148
Pomfret School, 97, 103
Pomfret United Agricultural Society, 21
Porter, Charles Ethan, 123
Potter, Judson A., 178
Prior, John, 20, 82
Putnam, 2, 25, 32, 38, 41, 53, 58, 64, 75, 76, 78,
    83, 85, 86, 89, 90, 92, 101, 119, 121, 122,
    123, 126, 135, 136, 139, 143, 148, 149, 15?,
    161, 163, 166, 172, 174, 182, 184
Putnam & Thompson Street Railroad
    Company, 78
Putnam Woolen Company, 41, 184
Putnam, Gen. Israel, 58, 142, 160

Q

Quebec Square, 51
Quinebaug Company, 45, 51
Quinebaug River, 25, 40, 149, 152, 153
Quinebaug Valley Community College,
    99, 105, 106

R

Rankin, Julia, 105
Recreation Park, 29, 51, 66, 67, 170
Red Cross, 161, 163
Reserve Officers' Training Corps (ROTC), 1?
Revolutionary War, 12, 160
Rhode Island Agricultural College, 144
Ribicoff, Abraham, 172
Richards, John, 136
Richmond, F. H., 178
Richmond, Perez, 36
Rieggers, William J., 185
Robinson, Johnny, 95
Rock Mill, 37
Rockville, 21, 22, 37, 58, 59, 63, 78, 119, 121,
    123, 135, 136, 138, 148, 162, 164
Rockville High School, 100
Rocky Point, Rhode Island, 86
Roosevelt, Eleanor, 165
Roosevelt, Franklin D., 121
Roosevelt, Theodore, 59, 66
Rose, E. P., 142
Roseland Cottage, 134, 137
Rotary Club, Willimantic, 65
Rufleth, Ed, 26
Rumanian Athletic Club, 123

S

Salle Union, 122
Sartorius, Ina, 99
Sayles, Henry, 27
Scenic Theatre, 135
Schuller, William, 22
Scotland, 36, 61, 102
Shaw, E. Burton, 42
Shea, Patrick J., 159
Shell Chateau Restaurant, 155
Sherman, Hy, 166
Shriver, Eunice Kennedy, 104
Sisters of Mercy, 101
Sisters of the Holy Ghost, 101
Slater, Samuel, 36
Sledjeski, William, 92
Smith, J. Eugene, 110
Smith, Queenie, 170, 176
Snow, Charles W., 178
Somers, 18, 21, 74, 84, 97, 171
Somers Creamery Company, 18
Somersville Manufacturing Company, 127

uth Coventry, 77, 88, 162
uth Village, 50
uth Willington, 36, 77, 88
uth Windham, 77, 88, 149, 155
uth Windham Volunteer Fire Department, 178
uth Woodstock, 58
uthbridge Local, 150
anish-American War, 159, 161
ink, Harvey, 25
iritualist Church, Somers, 127
iritualist Church, Willimantic, 131
 Edward's Church, Stafford, 66
 Jean Baptiste Society, 119, 121, 122
 Joseph's Church, Willimantic, 156,157
 Mary's Church, Putnam, 101,121
ifford, 21, 23, 26, 68, 77, 78, 89, 96, 97, 100, 119, 126, 135, 149, 150, 154, 155, 166, 174, 175, 176, 177, 179, 182, 184, 185. *See also* Stafford Springs, Staffordville
ifford Fair, 21, 28, 168
ifford Historical Society, 89
ifford Motor Speedway, 21, 28
ifford Springs, 66, 77, 78, 87, 88, 134, 137, 156, 181
ifford Springs Hotel, 28, 134
iffordville, 171
ndish, Edward K., 43
nley, George, 22
r Theatre, 135
ite Firemen's Muster and Parade, 64
rling, 27, 124. *See also* Oneco
mson, Rufus W., 111
rrs, 78, 80, 99, 163, 177
rrs Agricultural College. *See* University of Connecticut
rrs Agricultural School. *See* University of Connecticut
rrs, Augustus, 98
rrs, Charles, 98
rrs, Hector W., 162
dents Army Training Corps, 163
dents for a Democratic Society (SDS), 167
llivan, John L., 182
ift, Nathan, Jr., 186

ft, William Howard, 66, 67, 170
lcottville, 148
nner, Oscar, 135, 170, 182
ppan, Lewis, 98
shlik, Joe, 166
em, Charles, 141
ylor, George, 66
mple B'nai Israel, Willimantic, 131
nnis Club of Rockville, 138
nt City, 53
rry, Felicia, 107
atcher, James, 139
e Oaks, 51
ompson, 82, 116, 122, 133, 138. *See also* East Thompson, North Grosvenordale
read City Bottling Works, 182
read City Cyclers, 140
ssing, Captain H. E., 67
land, 21, 22, 59, 82, 96, 100, 149, 172
land Academy, 100
land County Agricultural Fair, 21
gue, Robert, 100
vn Hall, Willimantic, 151, 178
nity Episcopal Church, Brooklyn, 130

Truman, Harry S., 161
Trumbull, Jonathon, 160
Turnerville, 148
Turnverein, 119, 121
Twain, Mark, 123, 148

U

Union, 19, 20, 97, 99, 160, 170, 186
Union School, 99
Union Station, Stafford, 90
United Textile Workers of America, 53
University of Connecticut, 14, 33, 80, 98, 99, 104, 110, 112, 113, 114, 115, 136, 141, 144, 145, 163, 164, 165, 166, 167, 172, 177
Upton, John, 83
Utley, Carrie, 179

V

Venerable Club, 170, 179
Vernon, 58, 67, 135, 140, 148, 174. *See also* Rockville, Talcottville
Vietnam War, 163, 167
Villa, Pancho, 161
Vinton, Simeon O., 161
Vito, Tony, 82

W

Wabbaquasset Polo Club, 58
Walker, Burt, 171
Walsh, Mary, 185
War of 1812, 160
Warren, Florence, 141
Warren, William, 141
Warrenville, 129
Washington, George, 74, 82, 160
Wauregan, 37, 41, 50
Wauregan Mills, 39, 40, 42, 44, 46, 48, 49, 50, 149, 152, 166
Weir, J. Alden, 40
Welch, Fannie Dixon, 102, 172
West Street Cemetery, 179
West Street Social Eight, 170, 179
West Willington, 77, 88
Wheeler, Charles N. C., 143
Whitaker, Ernest C., 95
White House Cafe, 126
White Train, The, 89
Wilcox, Dr. George E., 140
Wildwood Park, 86
Willard, Dr. Samuel, 134
William Benton Museum of Art, 115
Willimantic, 29, 36, 37, 38, 39, 50, 51, 52, 53, 56, 58, 59, 60, 62, 64, 65, 66, 67, 68, 69, 70, 71, 74, 76, 77, 78, 80, 81, 83, 87, 88, 89, 90, 95, 98, 99, 101, 107, 118, 119, 120, 126, 127, 128, 130, 131, 134, 135, 136, 139, 140, 142, 144, 146,148, 149, 150, 151, 154, 155, 156, 157, 159, 161,163, 170, 172, 176, 178, 179, 180, 181
Willimantic Agricultural Fair, 29
Willimantic Camp Ground, 121, 128, 129
Willimantic Company, 162
Willimantic Linen Company. *See* American Thread Company
Willimantic Normal School. *See* Eastern Connecticut State University
Willimantic Railroad Station, 163
Willimantic River, 62, 70, 91, 151
Willimantic State College. *See* Eastern Connecticut State University
Willimantic State Teachers College. *See*

Eastern Connecticut State University
Willimantic Traction Company, 78, 87
Willimantic Urban Renewal Project, 65, 70, 130
Willington, 18, 74, 78, 79, 81, 96, 102, 149. *See also* South Willington, West Willington
Wilson, Kenneth, 115
Wilson, Woodrow, 161
Windham, 58, 118, 160, 161, 170. *See also* North Windham, South Windham, Willimantic, Windham Center
Windham Center, 60, 149
Windham Center Cemetery, 40
Windham Center Volunteer Fire Department, 178
Windham Concert Band, 143
Windham County Agricultural Society, 21
Windham High School, 81, 102, 153
Windham Historical Society, 71
Windham Manufacturing Company, 39
Windham Textile and History Museum, 37, 49, 55
Windham Town Hall, 65
Wolf Den, 142
Wood, George, 77, 181
Woodstock, 21, 58, 59, 131, 134, 137, 179. *See also* South Woodstock
Woodstock Academy, 59, 97, 103
Woodstock Fair, 31
Workmen's Circle, 101
World War I, 161, 162, 163, 164
World War II, 162, 163, 165, 166
Wright, Kenneth, 145

Y

Yale University, 98, 99, 136, 172
Yiddish School, 101
YMCA, Willimantic, 65

About the Authors

Bruce M. Stave is professor of history and chairman of the department at the University of Connecticut, where he is also director of the Center for Oral History.

He is author or editor of seven books including five in the field of urban history: *The New Deal and the Last Hurrah; Urban Bosses, Machines, and Progressive Reformers; Socialism and The Cities; The Making of Urban History: Historiography Through Oral History;* and *Modern Industrial Cities: History, Policy, and Survival.*

Stave is the general editor of the University Publications of America series, *Research Collections in Urban History and Urban Studies.* He is associate editor of the *Journal of Urban History,* which since 1974 has published twenty of his oral history conversations with leading urban historians. These deal with the development of the field in the United States, Great Britain, France, Canada, Australia, Sweden, and the People's Republic of

China. He serves as a director of the Urban History Association. He has edited a special issue of the *Journal* on "Photography & Urban History" (May 1989).

Stave has been a Fulbright professor at Peking University in Beijing, People's Republic of China (1984-85), where he taught American urban history. He also has held Fulbright awards in New Zealand, Australia, and the Philippines (1977), and in India (1968-1969) as well as lecturing abroad in England, Iceland, Sweden, Kenya, Turkey, Indonesia, Nepal, and Canada.

He has been a National Endowment for the Humanities fellow and a Mellon Pre-doctoral fellow. He is a former president of the New England Association of Oral History and has been a member of the Board of Directors of the Connecticut Humanities Council and the New England Foundation for the Humanities. He lives in Coventry, Connecticut.

Michele Palmer, a resident of Storrs, Connecticut, is manager of Tapescribe, the transcribing service of the Center for Oral History at the University of Connecticut. She participated in the Center's Connecticut Workers and Technological Change oral history project, writing a series of radio scripts based on the project for Connecticut Public Radio. A former newspaper reporter, as well as editor and publisher of a small press, Ms. Palmer is also a freelance writer. She is the author of several children's books and numerous stories and articles for magazines. Besides writing, Ms. Palmer pursues an interest in art, through her own work as an artist and as a docent at the William Benton Museum of Art. She is a graduate of the University of Pennsylvania.

Along the Line

PUBLISHED FOR MEMBERS & FRIENDS OF THE RAILROAD MUSEUM OF NEW ENGLAND

VOLUME 24, NUMBER 1   BILL SAMPLE, EDITOR   JANUARY-FEBRUARY 1991

The tractor-trailer rig has pulled into position for unloading GE loco #3 onto the Museum Yard track. The locomotive was a tight fit for the trailer.   H. Pincus photo

LINES EAST....

THE "NEW CRITTER" ARRIVES AT WILLIMANTIC

Once upon a time the RMNE was donated a "critter", i. e. a small industrial diesel locomotive. While the donation of this locomotive was gratefully accepted, it really didn't fit into the museum's planning at the time and it was decided that the new acquisition would be sold to provide needed cash for other restoration projects. Arrangements were made, and that first critter was soon polishing the iron of the Old Colony and Newport, a scenic tourist railway in Rhode Island, and all parties were content.

A few years later, things were different- the RMNE had made the decision to eventually relocate from the Valley Railroad property to its own facility at Willimantic. At our new site we would not have the services of Valley and U S Army Reserve motive power to perform our switching needs, and while we have two serviceable locomotives with a third on the way they are Big Locomotives and not the most economical choices for use for an occasion-

al switching move. The answer to this upcoming dilemma was to obtain another critter.

The vast resources of the RMNE were put to work in obtaining a suitable locomotive. Luck was with us as word was eventually received that a 45 ton industrial switcher might be available in eastern Massachusetts. The location was the River Works of General Electric, a vast industrial complex straddling the Eastern line of the Boston & Maine Railroad near Lynn. The use of rail service was drawing to a close as GE was shifting away from the steam turbine manufacturing at that location in favor of jet engine production, which has little need for rail. The locomotive, number 3, was the last of four that had been built for use at the River Works in 1942 to replace electrically powered locomotives that had probably worked there since the plant was constructed in the teens. Seeing only sporadic use in recent years, #3 had last been observed in use about a year ago, hauling an outbound load of scrap by employee Bill Crawford, who is the president of the Massachusetts Bay division of the Railroad Enthusiasts. It was Bill who helped to arrange the donation of the critter after hearing of the RMNE's needs from trustee Louie Edmonds. Although the locomotive had earlier been slated to go to another GE facility in Rutland, VT as part of a proposed commuter service, we were the winner after the Vermont project was dropped. By last September negotiations began in earnest, and during the fall the locomotive was inspected by Howard Pincus, Dave Kornfeld and Bill Jeske who agreed that it was in excellent condition and would be well suited for our needs.

Following the completion of the donation, it was time to arrange the transport of #3 to Willimantic. John Shaughnessy of Shaughnessy Trucking, a rigging specialist, was called in; and our own Dick Joos of Northern Division fame took charge of coordinating the move from start to finish. The mode of transport would be a heavy duty tractor-trailer combination.

Meanwhile, arrangements were being made being made back in Willimantic to receive our new critter. The far end of the yard was selected as the unloading point, and a fenced compound was contemplated for a storage area. Construction began at both points, with an excavation at the track's end and fencing on the house track lead being completed by Bill Jeske's crew. While this was underway, loading plans at the River Works were finalized.

Friday, December 14, was the big day for the move. Rail was attached to the trailer bed, and this was temporarily attached to a siding that had been jacked up to serve as a ramp. Although it was originally proposed to winch #3 onto the trailer, the lack of a winch truck caused plan B to go into effect: start up the locomotive and run it onto the trailer under its own power. This was accomplished successfully, the cargo was secured to the trailer and the locomotive said farewell to its home for almost a half century. A long, slow journey followed as the 45 ton #3 made its way to a new home, finally arriving there at about 7:00pm. This task was much more difficult than it appears as much paperwork had to be completed for the oversized load, but thanks to Dick Joos and truck owner-operator Dick Butler the trip was run successfully. But there were problems with the unloading site!

Anyone who has visited our Willimantic site knows that the access road is far from smooth, and smooth surfaces are a must for a low riding trailer with a good 45 tons planted on it. It was quickly discovered that the crossing of the house track lead was an obstacle, so an alternate plan was hastily devised. The new unloading point was the end of the house track, easily accessible from the recently rebuilt parking lot of the River Club restaurant. Some work was required to prepare the end of that track, this being directed by Tom Briggs, who borrowed a front end loader from the owner of the River Club. Meanwhile the eastern end of the "critter pen", a fenced off security area for #3, had to be dismantled. The track itself was ready, having received 12 new ties installed by Bill Jeske and company. As noon approached on Saturday, December 15 the unloading ramp was ready, connected to the trailer's rails. The locomotive to trailer tie downs were removed, the locomotive's engines were fired up and soon #3 was ready to make its maiden journey onto New England Railroad iron. With RMNE Chairman and President Howard Pincus at the throttle and the locomotive's and the town's noon whistle blowing under a rainy sky, our New Critter crept off the trailer onto solid trackage. The Railroad Museum of New England had moved another step down the long road to the development of our new home.

This event's successful conclusion was accomplished thanks to many members and friends of the RMNE. Louie Edmonds worked with Bill Crawford and A. D. English of General Electric to make the donation a reality. Bill also helped in another way by arranging a donation of $1000. from the Mass Bay Railroad Enthusiasts to help with moving expenses. Dick Joos gets a big tip of the hat for directing the movement from start to finish. Bill Jeske, Tom Briggs and the Lines East crew at Willimantic worked tirelessly and sometimes under horrible weather conditions to prepare the site and assist with the unloading.

OTHER LINES EAST NEWS

Most of the recent site work has been preparing the area for the arrival of GE #3, readying the house track lead and security compound. The security compound itself has an historic precedent a number of miles to the west: During the final years of the Connecticut Company's former trolley freight line in East Hartford, their motive power was kept in such a pen adjacent to the former New York & New England main line.

Once again, many local businesses have been most generous in their support of the RMNE. Recent donations have included the use of the front end loader from the River Club as previously mentioned, fencing assistance and two gates from Roger Hence of the Hence Fence Company, the use of an auger truck for fence post digging by Connecticut Light & Power and driver Curt Dowling, and 20 used telephone poles from the Southern New England Telephone Company.

Even with the colder weather the turnout at Willimantic has been continually growing. Work crews approaching 20 volunteers are becoming common. Recent participants have included Bob and Rob Nejako, Art Hall, Joe Cerreto, Mike O'Donnell, Howard Bidwell, Bill Breadheft, Brian Wagner, Dan Ditulio, Morgan Steele, Brian Hakey, Bill Sample, Howard Pincus, Dave Dziomba, Dick Joos, Patt Sekula, Tom and Carole Briggs, Jim Beeler, Bill Jeske and many other interested local residents.

Bill Jeske, Howard Pincus and Art Hall attended a meeting of the Windham Selectmen on December 18. The Selectmen proclaimed that the 1990s would be the "Decade of the Railroad Museum of New England" and we received an official document to that effect. Our members present brought the town up to date on RMNE activities. Also, the possibility of a storefront office in Willimantic is being investigated.

STACK TALK: RMNE NEWS

LOCOMOTIVES AND ROLLING STOCK

NH #0401, ALCO FA1

Back in the Saybrook yard, the major project continues to be the resurrection of our famous Alco cab unit. The locomotive has been "winterized"- the large roof hatch has been temporarily reinstalled, the small hatch has been covered with a framework supporting a clear plastic tarp, providing a skylight of sorts and the sides have been temporarily enclosed with plywood and tarps. A diaphragm of sorts will soon be construct to provide a weather tight opening between the locomotive and parts car W-221. Wooden cable clamps were manufactured by our woodworking shop's George Wisner and Walt Hermann, painted and installed in the cable troughs. The main generator to traction motor cable (previously donated by Brand-Rex of Willimantic) has been about 90% installed, and access openings in the trough have been sealed by welding. Most of the painting in the carbody interior has been completed, some touch up will be required when the weather warms up a bit. Metalwork is also being attended to in the cab area. Another job keeping crews busy is the priming and painting of the many disassembled pieces (piping, etc.) from the engine room. Those observed recently working on the 0401 have been Eli Ellis, Jon Chase, John Mitchell, Howard Pincus, Doug Kydd, Bob Hart and Bill Sample.

NH #17219, 17221 Flat Cars

A project not heard from for awhile, these cars (donated by the Farrel Corporation of Ansonia) have been overhauled for shipment to Willimantic. A third car of the same series, which had been removed from its trucks, has been scrapped after sales attempts were unsuccessful, with some parts, including the trucks, being saved.

Arrivals and Departures

It appears most of the fleet of former New Haven 8600 series cars has been sold. In addition, former electric multiple unit combine NH 4670 is likely to be included in that sale. These cars are reportedly heading for the west coast for service on a tourist railway. Two 8600s will be kept by the RMNE.

Arrangements are being made to obtain the former "Westport"' a one time New Haven heavyweight parlor car last used in work train service as the W-943. The car currently resides in New Haven, behind the diesel shop.

TRACK DEPARTMENT

A large effort to obtain unused rail, switches and other track hardware is currently underway. Working with the state of Connecticut Department of Transportation, much material has been lined up and some is already enroute to Willimantic. Also, track removal projects in Massachusetts continue.

Willimantic Yard crew is busy replacing ties on the old freight house track, in preparation for the arrival of GE loco #3. November 1990 photo by H. Pincus

THE LATEST ON THE BRADLEY COLLECTION

The movement of our cars from the Jim Bradley estate is getting closer. A cooperative effort has been established with the Valley Railroad Company as they have obtained the parlor car "Great Republic" from Jim's collection. (The remaining two cars, former observation-lounge "Fox Point" and sleeper "Breslin Tower" have not been sold as of January 1991. VRRCo and RMNE personnel have been studying access routes and getting quotes from rigging companies concerning the move. We have recently purchased 12 wheelsets for installation where needed on our "Stag Hound",

"Philinda" and "Forest Hills" cars, and a grant from the state of Connecticut to help with the move is pending.

PRESENTING THE 1991 BOARD OF TRUSTEES....

The Board of Trustees consists of Howard Pincus, Bob Hart, Nancy Peacos, Al Galanty, Hal Reiser, Louie Edmonds, Fred Carstensen and newly elected Bob Bass and Bill Sample. The RMNE thanks former board members Jon Chase and Bill Dulmaine for their service during 1990.

November 17, 1990: The first replacement power cables are pulled into #0401's nose door and into position in the engine room. The cable was donated by Brand-Rex Co. of Willimantic. Photo by H. Pincus

CABOOSE CHATTER

Dues notices are now being mailed. Please pay yours promptly as we wish to keep both the Membership Chairman and Treasurer happy!

Whoops...we forgot to mention one of last fall's activities was another weekend at The Big E, the Eastern States Exposition in W. Springfield, Mass. We had an excellent location in the Connecticut Building, thanks to the work of Mike Robinson. Printouts of excepts from previous newsletters were available, and many people were educated on who we were and what we were doing. There was a good turnout of volunteer support: assisting Mike were wife Bonnie and daughter Kathryn, Ed and Rosa Robinson, Bill Sample, John Schneider, and Nancy Peacos.

The entire 1205th Railway Services Unit, U S Army Reserve has been called to active duty due to the current Persian Gulf situation. Several RMNE members, including your editor, will soon be journeying south. As this means some lost volunteer hours, please try to pitch in and help take up the slack. There is a busy show season coming up, and Al Galanty will need a new assistant for the duration.

For now, the mail drop for the RMNE Southern Division will be Bill Sample, c/o Spivey, Rt 5 Box 235-c, Southport, NC 28461 Thanks to the following for their help with this issue: Bill Jeske, Howard Pincus, Bill Crawford, Bob Bass and Nancy Peacos.
...................................Sgt Bill Sample, Editor.

```
RMNE Message Phone (203) 395-0615
Howard Pincus     (914) 761-5286 after 7PM
Al Galanty        (203) 929-7745    "    "
Jon Chase         (203) 848-8008    "    "
Bill Jeske        (203) 742-9425    "    " (Wilmntic)
Louie Edmonds     (617) 862-0748    "    " (Boston)
Bill Sample       (203) 635-1464    "    "
```

ORDER BOARD

January	19	**All Member Work Day, Saybrook Yard, 9:30am.**
	20	Old Colony and Fall River Train Show, Armory, Fall River, Mass.
February	1	Mystic Valley RR Society Train Show, Dedham, Mass.
	9	Amherst Railway Society Train Show (the Big One), Exposition Grounds, W. Springfield, Mass.
	9	General Membership Meeting, Congregational Church Hall, Main St., Old Saybrook 5:30pm.
	10	Amherst Rwy. Society Train Show (cont'd).
	16	**All Member Work Day, Saybrook Yard, 9:30am.**
	24	Train Show, Civic Center, Old Greenwich, Ct.
March	2	Mass Bay RRE Railfan Excursion, from Boston.
	3	Fairfield (Ct) Train Show, Tomlinson School.
	9	General Membership Meeting and **Annual Dinner**, Radisson Hotel, New London. See flyer for details.
	10	Train Show, Mother Seton High School, Clark, NJ.
	16	**All Member Work Day, Saybrook Yard, 9:30am.**
	17	Cheshire High School Train Show, Cheshire, Ct.
	24	Kingston Model RR Club Train Show, Kingston, NY

The Railroad Museum of New England

P.O. BOX 97 • ESSEX, CT 06426

**FORWARDING AND ADDRESS
CORRECTION REQUESTED**

FIRST CLASS MAIL

Along the Line

PUBLISHED FOR MEMBERS & FRIENDS OF THE RAILROAD MUSEUM OF NEW ENGLAND

Volume 23, Number 8   Bill Sample, Editor   November-December 1990

Museum member Harry Malone steam cleaning the Model 244-H Alco V-12 diesel engine from NH #0401. The engine puts out 1600 horsepower and weighs 16 tons. The large round object on the right is the turbocharger. August 1990 photo by Dave Kornfeld

ORDER BOARD

December 2 Mohawk & Hudson Train Show, Albany, NY.

**December 8 Annual Meeting, Congregational Church Hall
          Main Street, Old Saybrook, CT 5:30pm.
          ELECTIONS!!!**
December 12 Weekday Work Night, Saybrook Yard, 5:00pm.
December 15 **All Member Work Day, Saybrook Yard.**
December 26 Weekday Work Night, Saybrook Yard, 5:00pm.

January   12 General Membership Meeting, Congregational
              Church Hall, Main St., Old Saybrook, 5:30pm

January   19 **All Member Work Day, Saybrook Yard.**
January   20 Old Colony & Fall River Train Show,
              Fall River Armory.

STACK TALK: RMNE NEWS

LINES EAST

The present appearance of the Air Line yard area is vastly different than what appeared during the early part of the summer. Work during early fall has completed the clearing of the yard, adjacent right of way, and some of the access road.

Following the first pass of heavy cutting of trees and brush that took place during the summer, in September chain and buck saws were replaced with mowers and string trimmers. An army of volunteers scoured the yard area, cutting the remaining vegetation right to the ground. Next, removal of the roadside fence was begun, and by early October removal in the yard area was about 75% completed.

The years of abandonment saw a very considerable amount of trash accumulate on the site area. While the town has been excellent at removing abandoned vehicles, smaller items in overgrown areas were still much in evidence, especially following the brush cutting. Therefore a general clean up day was held on October 20. Once again the generosity of local businesses was of great assistance. James DeVivo of Willimantic Waste Paper donated the use of a dumpster and the town of Windham waived tipping fees at the landfill. Virtually all trash was removed from the entry road, Air Line Yard, and the roundhouse site, where the turntable pit had become sort of a stone lined trash bin.

Presently work continues on the fence dismantling, with parts of it being recycled into an enclosure for a track material storage yard. With all existing trackage now cleared, repair work there will soon begin.

Members are encouraged to come to take a look at our future. You won't be disappointed! We can always use your assistance. Workdays are currently scheduled for every other Sunday. Phone Bill Jeske for details.

A big thank you for all who are making this project a success. Members helping during the past few months have included Howard Bidwell, Morgan Steele, Bob and Rob Nejako, Howard Brock, Tom and Carole Briggs, Brian Hakey, Dan Ditulio, Brian Wagner, Paul Webster, Bill Breadheft, Art Hall and Bill Jeske.

In other Lines East news, the first car of the RMNE fleet has arrived. Maine Central #17080, a 40 foot low side gondola car appeared in the Central Vermont's Willimantic yard around the 1st of November. This car was rescued from Boston, where it was in maintenance of way service (the previous service of many a preserved car) Part of a 150 car order, the car was built in August 1939.

LOCOMOTIVES AND ROLLING STOCK

NH 0401 Alco FA-1

Once again there is much progress to report in the restoration of our future pride and joy. As scheduled, sandblasting was performed over the fall by contractors (Dan Pluta and company), a move that saved many volunteer hours needed elsewhere. Dan and his assistant Roger also completed priming of the bare metal. Much of the carbody was completed, including the interior and exterior of the engine room. Eventually the nose interior and the cab and nose exterior were also blasted and primed by a combination of paid and volunteer labor. The areas of the locomotive untouched by the sandblast crews will eventually be needle scaled and sanded prior to finish painting. Sandblasting was also done to a number of loose parts of the locomotive.

Following the completion of the interior priming various tasks aiding further restoration were attended to. A plywood hatch was built to cover the radiator fan grill, and a framework was built to cover the roof hatch area prior to tarping. Temporary lighting was installed throughout the interior, a move necessary to combat earlier sunsets. The cleaning of the engine block was completed, and various components were spot primed.

Sandblasting the interior of the nose and cab areas of NH #0401 was completed by Howard Pincus and Hal Reiser on October 6. This photo of the nose shows the supplied-air hood used by the sandblast operator. Photo by Hal Reiser

At the present time the major project is finish painting the interior of the carbody. To date, the project is advancing from rear to front of the 0401, with at least two coats being necessary. Work will continue throughout the winter as the locomotive will be enclosed with provision for heating.

Workers on the project have included Bob Hart,

Howard Pincus, Jon Chase, Tom Brown, Hal Reiser, John Kiniry, Howard Beale, Mike O'Donnell, Dave Kornfeld, Bob Bass, and Bill Sample.

NH 3008 Wood Shop Car

George Wisner and Walt Hermann have continued fitting out this car, recently installing a wood and coal burning stove and stovepipe by the east door of the car. George says that he will have plenty of wood scraps in stock for the winter heating season.

FGEX 36026 Refrigerator Car

Thanks to the help of many, the exterior of the car has now received its final coat of paint, including exposed parts of the underbody. Lettering has been started but has been difficult due to the wooden siding's surface. The car is sitting a bit higher on its springs these days thanks to the use of a good percentage of the sandblast sand stored inside.

COMMUNICATION AND SIGNAL DEPARTMENT

As signal towers in southern New England continue on their march toward extinction, the RMNE is there to pick up some of the pieces. Former New Haven RR towers SS (signal station) 55 (Burr Road, near Bridgeport) and SS 214 (Hart) near Hartford have been removed from service, but pieces will survive in our collection. Under the guidance of RMNE signal czar Mike Robinson a good chunk of the SS55

"armstrong" interlocking machine was removed and transported to Saybrook. Later visits by Mike netted several different types of signal relays. The accumulated materials were placed in B&M 1910, the assigned signal department car. Assisting on the SS55 project were Phil Paradis, Bill Sample, Jeff Blaisdell, Ray Giddings, and Dick Joos.

SAYBROOK YARD HAPPENINGS

"George's Crossing" has recently been completed by George Wisner and Walt Hermann. This is a wooden crossing on track 9 opposite the wood shop car, greatly improving accessibility.

The next crossing project will be over the north end of track 13, allowing access to the "back yard" storage area.

Our Ford boom truck has recently received major servicing thanks to the cooperation of the Connecticut Central Railroad. Included in the repair work was the replacement of a broken exhaust manifold and the installation of a new fuel gauge, which will be most appreciated on our longer trips.

DONATIONS

The RMNE gratefully acknowledges the donation of trucking services (for the SS55 project) and a load of coal from Mike Sloan's Berkshire Petroleum.

We have also been awarded a grant from the state of Connecticut toward the movement of the Bradley cars. Details will follow in an upcoming issue.

Hal Reiser priming the cab interior of NH #0401 after sandblasting was completed. October 7 photo by H. Pincus

SALES DEPARTMENT

We are now approximately halfway through the train show season. Results have been a bit slower than last year, most likely due to the current economic recession. To counter this we are now accepting Master Card and Visa credit cards, with a $50.00 minimum purchase, which immediately was reflected in our sales totals. We have also taken our wares as far away as Gaithersburg, Md., a two day event attended by people and dealers from as far away as Texas and Wisconsin. Al Galanty has tirelessly headed up this effort, assisted by Jim Carlson, Carl Weber and Bill Sample. Any additional help will be appreciated.

Coming soon: RMNE t-shirts!

CABOOSE CHATTER

The 1990 Railway Preservation Symposium at the Railroad Museum of Pennsylvania was attended by Howard Pincus, Jon Chase, Tom Brown and Bill Sample. As in last year's event, the 1990 edition was both informative and entertaining. As in 1989, we also visited Steamtown in Scranton on our way to Strasburg, noting the progress that has been over the past year.

PRR 108448, a steel X26 box car, has been sold. This car has been stored off site, and now can be removed from your roster.

Duty Calls: The 1205th Railway Services Unit of the Army Reserve has been partially activated to help support the current Persian Gulf buildup. To date members Mike Hanna, Brian Hakey and Bill Sample have been assigned to assist rail operations at Military Ocean Terminal Sunny Point near Southport, NC. The 1205th is a descendent of the old 729th Railway Operating Battalion, a unit once sponsored by the New Haven Railroad which saw service in the European theater of World War II and in Korea.

Thanks to the following for their assistance with this issue: W Jeske, N Peacos, H Pincus and W Dulmaine.

Sgt Bill Sample, Editor.

CVRM/RMNE Message Phone (203) 395-0615
Howard Pincus (914) 761-5286 after 7:00 p.m.
Al Galanty (203) 929-7745 after 5:00 p.m.
Jon Chase (203) 848-8008 after 7:00 p.m.

The Railroad Museum of New England

P.O. BOX 97 • ESSEX, CT 06426

**FORWARDING AND ADDRESS
CORRECTION REQUESTED**

FIRST CLASS MAIL

Along the Line

PUBLISHED FOR MEMBERS & FRIENDS OF THE RAILROAD MUSEUM OF NEW ENGLAND

Volume 23, Number 7   BILL SAMPLE, EDITOR   September-October 1990

Interior of 1903 wood baggage car NH 3844, after removal of seats stored in car. Restoration work will be starting on this car

ORDER BOARD

October	7	Train Show, Exposition Grounds, W. Springfield.
	10	Weekday Work Night, Saybrook Yard, 5:00 p.m.
	13	General Membership Meeting, Congregational Church Hall, Main St., Old Saybrook, 6:30 p.m.
	20	ALL MEMBER WORK DAY, SAYBROOK YARD, 9:00 a.m.
	21	Train Show, New London.
	24	Weekday Work Night, Saybrook Yard, 5:00 p.m.
November	4	Train Show, Gaithersburg, MD.
	10	NHRHTA Train Show and Reunion, Ramada Inn, North Haven. GENERAL MEMBERSHIP MEETING POSTPONED TO NOVEMBER 17!!!
	11	Westchester County Train Show, White Plains, NY.
	14	Weekday Work Night, Saybrook Yard, 5:00 p.m.
	17	ALL MEMBER WORK DAY, SAYBROOK YARD, 9:00 a.m.
	17	GENERAL MEMBERSHIP MEETING, NOMINATIONS FOR BOARD OF TRUSTEES, Congregational Church Hall, Main St., Old Saybrook, 5:30 p.m. (please note our new Winter meeting time)
	18	Train Show, Cheshire High School.
	28	Train Show, St. Vincent de Paul Hall, Elmont, NY.

IMPORTANT NOTICE:

NOVEMBER MEETING — RESCHEDULED TO NOV. 17!
Three positions on the board of trustees will be open for nomination. Please plan to attend this important meeting.

Museum member Jay Stone painting FGEX refrigerator car at Saybrook Yard, H. Pincus photo

Support Your Sales Department: Patronize the Museum Store at Essex and the RMNE tables at the above shows.

Chairperson Nancy Peacos of the Annual Dinner Committee is seeking assistance and suggestions for the 1991 event. Please contact Nancy at (203) 859-3548.

PROJECT 0401
by Dave Kornfeld

During the past month, activities on Alco FA1 NH 0401 have virtually reached a fever pitch. After a great deal of effort, it can be safely stated that the steam cleaning of the chassis has been completed. The addition of a new steam cleaner helped this immeasurably, along with the usual hand scraping and shoveling of debris. The steam cleaner has also been applied in the cleaning of the diesel engine in order to remove a good seventeen years of accumulated grime.

Over the course of a long Saturday, members Don McCra and John Kiniry attended to the thankless task of cleaning out the crankcase of the model 244 engine. First, the screens were removed from the crankcase via the inspection hatches. These screens served as barriers to prevent debris, in the form of failed bearings and other metallic parts from entering the lube oil system. In the course of operation, sludge also tends to accumulate on these screens, possibly masking serious problems. The screens were cleaned with diesel fuel and restored to like-new condition. Following this, the interior of the crankcase was cleaned out to remove sludge and any condensation from the engine base. Wrapping things up, the screens were reinstalled and the entire area was given a coating of lube oil to prevent any possible rust buildup. The used diesel fuel was retained in 55 gallon drums for later disposal.

As has been the case over the past several months, Eli Ellis has continued his efforts in the fabricating department. The operator's cab is rounding into shape, and will be ready for reassembly this winter. Eli also burned off some rotted cooling system piping that had been welded into place. Replacement for this will be fabricated on-site and reinstalled this fall.

It can also be safely stated that both carbody sides are now ready for sandblasting and priming. All remaining clamping strips, screening, door casings and other miscellaneous assemblies have been removed for repair and reapplication or for scrapping. This leaves just the frame structure, which resembles a truss-type bridge. Through the efforts of Jon Chase and Pat Fahey, a plywood curtain wall has been begun to contain sandblast grit. This same plywood will later be recycled to the exterior of the carbody to serve as a wintertime enclosure, allowing interior work to continue during the colder months. To speed up the project, this sandblasting will be done primarily by contract labor.

Lastly, preparation for the reassembly phase of the project has been intensifying. The matter of the failed eddy current clutch/gear unit has been dealt with. For the benefit of the uninitiated, the function of the eddy current clutch/gear unit is to drive the large cooling fan located in the aft portion of the locomotive. The Green Bay and Western Railroad Company, one of the last remaining citadels of Alco diesel-electric locomotives, has been engaged to repair this item. A pair of the correct traction motor blowers has been located in Brazil. Arrangements are in process to trade some surplus Amplidyne panels to the owners of the blowers, who are a group of railway enthusiasts.

And finally, former Alco Service Manager C.G. MacDermot has been retained to consult on various aspects of the reassembly process. Believe it or not, Mr. MacDermot has a previous connection with this particular locomotive, as he was the Alco service engineer who placed it in service following its 1959 factory rebuilding.

STACK TALK:
RMNE NEWS

As we enter the Autumn of 1990, we find several different work crews toiling on various RMNE projects at various locations in New

England. Informally, your editor and others have given names to these groups. If members actively participating in the various "divisions" have better suggestions, please let your editor know!

LINES EAST

Several important events have transpired concerning the Willimantic site and future operations:

First, Willimantic Yardmaster, Bill Jeske has proudly announced that "Tracks Are Back" (in sight) in the former Air Line Yard, north of Bridge St. During the summer, permission was formally granted to the RMNE by the state Department of Transportation to occupy and improve the remaining Air Line Yard trackage. This area was last used for box car storage by the Providence and Worcester Railroad during the early 1980s, and even then, the brush was growing a bit heavy. By 1990, much of the 3 track yard had disappeared into the lush foliage. Enter Bill Jeske and his regular crew of Howard Brock, Howard Bidwell and Morgan Steele and soon the maple, oak and even poison ivy began to succumb to saws, axes and loppers. At various times, others such as Brian Hakey; Danny Brock; Rob and Bob Nejako; Mike O'Donnel; Dave Dziomba and Bill Sample have participated, plus a number of local residents (future members) who have assisted due to their interest in the success of the project. The result: all of the existing trackage has been cleared and the brush hauled away, thanks to the efforts of a local farmer who donated two grain trucks for the job. The weed control has been applied to the area, and the next job is to mark the ties needing replacement.

A second newsworthy event was the establishment of our operating subsidiary, the New England Railroad Company. The NERRCo was established to oversee the railroad operations of the RMNE per the wishes of the state of Connecticut, much like the Valley Railroad Company was at the beginning of that operation. Our operation will differ from the VRR in a number of ways, the most important being only one share of stock will be issued and that will be owned by the RMNE. Most of the work going into this important phase of our history was done by member, Carole Briggs and her secretary, Mary.

Thirdly, much time has already been spent in setting up the framework of the NERRCo operation, thanks to Bob Bass. Officials are being recruited, primarily those who are currently professionally employed in the railroad industry. An operating timetable is being produced, and it has been decided that we will operate under NORAC rules, the rules currently being used by virtually all northeastern railroad operations.

NORTHERN DIVISION

This division has been quietly hard at work on projects in New Hampshire and Vermont since last spring. The participants to date have been Al Pomeroy and Dick Joos, plus virtually all members of Dick's family. The major project for this group is a recently obtained former Boston & Maine double sheathed wooden box car, lately the property of the Claremont & Concord Railroad at Claremont Jct. This United States Railway Administration type car was built around 1919, a representative of thousands of cars built for many railroads from a standard design. The car will replace a sister car at Essex (B&M 70466) which is in poor condition and will be disposed of.

Springtime saw the final arrangements made to obtain the B&M car, as well as a former Rock Island car. The cars, both about half loaded, had their contents gone over and sorted by Dick and daughters, Susie and Barbara, as well as Rick Gassett. Around this time, Al Pomeroy completed a rebuilding of the B&M car's air brake system. A local contractor, George Smith, got involved with the project and helped swap the trucks between the two cars, generously providing a heavy-duty forklift and an employee to assist with the job. Dick, Susie and Al were also in on this phase of the project. As the RMNE wasn't interested in the RI car, George took it off our hands and off the C&C property, leaving us with a cash contribution instead of an unwanted car.

During the summer, the final phase of mechanical work was completed. Damaged center plates were repaired, and offset side bearing pedestals were fabricated by Dick and his son, Butch, at the shop of Henniker Truck and Trailer, in nearby Henniker, NH, and installed the same day. The final job, repacking the journal bearing boxes, was completed by Al. The car has now been stenciled and awaits

Jon Chase working on the threshold area under the side door, FGEX refrigerator car #36026. H. Pincus photo

inspection before movement off the Claremont and Concord.

Also during the summer, Dick and his wife Joan travelled to St. Albans, VT, where a pair of air jacks that had been donated by the Central Vermont Railway were waiting. Dick and Joan loaded the jacks, and they are now safely on RMNE property.

CENTRAL MASSACHUSETTS DIVISION

Dave Jodoin, Ernie Gatzke and John Mrazik form the nucleus of this group, which will help to feed salvaged track material from the Worcester area to Willimantic. Several potential projects have been examined, and currently track removal has begun on a disused spur at a paper mill. Work such as this, will be very important for the development of the Willimantic site.

MINUTEMAN DIVISION

Louie Edmonds and crew has kept busy over the summer on their salvage of a spur to the Hanscom Air Force Base. To date, over 1,000 feet of brush has been cleared, and over 600 feet of rail has been lifted. The crew has been meeting about four times a month. Contact Louie for further details.

LOCOMOTIVES AND ROLLING STOCK

NH 529, Alco RS3
The locomotive was recently cranked up and idled as part of its annual exercise. A pre-lubrication system was used, an important item for engines that are rarely used. The 529 attracted considerable attention from Valley Railroad visitors.

NH 0401, Alco FA1
The latest news (as of late September) has the sandblasting just about completed. A recent visit saw the carbody in primer from the cab back, and the sandblast crew reported the unmasking of several color schemes in the process. The engine room interior is also completed, and it is now the time for reassembly.

Thanks to the following for their help with this issue: Dave Kornfeld; Bill Jeske; Howard Pincus and Bill Dulmaine.
.... *Bill Sample, Editor*

The Railroad Museum of New England
P.O. BOX 97 • ESSEX, CT 06426

**FORWARDING AND ADDRESS
CORRECTION REQUESTED**

FIRST CLASS MAIL

The Railroad Museum of New England

P.O. Box 97
Essex, CT 06426

The following articles have recently appeared in "ALONG THE LINE", the newsletter of the Railroad Museum of New England. They are reprinted here to acquaint you with the RMNE and our plans for the future.

Membership applications may be obtained from E.B.Robinson, 587 West St., Southington, CT. 06489.

It Will Be Willimantic!!

9/89

By Bill Sample

Following over two years of exhaustive study, the CVRM Site Development Committee has found a location that will allow our organization to realize our goal of establishing a complete regional railroad museum. This was not a decision that was taken lightly as literally thousands of volunteer hours and dollars have been spent on the subject. Meetings were held at various locations across the state with government officials (state and local), operating railroads, and museum organizations. Locations such as Danbury, Waterbury, New Haven, East Hartford, New London, and, of course, the Valley Railroad property were scrutinized, narrowed down and investigated further. While we received enthusiastic support from a couple of the finalists, none could top the welcome and potential offered at Willimantic.

Jon Chase stated a number of needs to create a successful Railroad Museum of New England in his report and Willimantic has already addressed two of the most important. Specifically, a most suitable site has been examined: some 32 acres of publicly-owned property that was once the site of the New Haven Railroad's Willimantic yard and engine terminal. From this point, trains departed for such points as New Haven, Hartford, Waterbury, Boston and Providence, while the trains of the Central Vermont Railway passed adjacent to the site enroute to New London or points north. The site presently contains three yard tracks, the remnant of the Hartford main line, and the easily observed grades of the Air Line, wye track, and the foundations of various engine terminal buildings. The site is well graded, well drained and accessible.

While a good site is most important, community support is what makes getting that site possible. The preliminary signal received from the town of Windham, of which the community of Willimantic is part, is definitely a "green board." First, Selectman Norman R. French of Windham recently stated that the proposed railroad museum would have a most important impact on downtown Willimantic, and together with the about-to-open Windham Textile and History Museum, will bring a new influx of people into the downtown area.

We are moving to survive. We must all realize that the interests of the Valley and the CVRM have diverged — the Valley is a tourist railway, and we are a railroad museum. To fund the projects of our museum's activities, we must have the ability to generate sufficient revenues from such sources as admissions, concessions and donations — something that is not possible on someone else's property. It is our desire to create a new attraction that will create increased tourism to the state, thus benefiting all.

Lines East

On November 8 at the Windham Town Hall in Willimantic, another important step in the development of the Railroad Museum of New England took place. The final lease agreement for the museum site was approved 9-1 by the board of selectmen and signed by CVRM Chairman Howard Pincus and Windham First Selectman Norman French. The leased property includes about 37 acres bounded roughly by Bridge Street, the former Hartford line, and the Willimantic River. Terms of the lease: 99 years at $1.00 per year, with the CVRM carrying $2 million in liability insurance. The CVRM has the right to sublet parts of the property providing the use is museum related.

An initial meeting between the CVRM and the Central Vermont Railway was held recently in Palmer. Both parties discussed future operating plans in the Willimantic area, and pledged cooperation in the formation of an official operating agreement. The CV was very receptive to our plans, and it will be a pleasure working with them.

CVRM OR RMNE: WHO ARE WE, REALLY?

8/90

Over the course of the past year plus, our members have seen the old Connecticut Valley Railroad Museum name being phased out, replaced with the Railroad Museum of New England title. This may be a bit confusing to some, especially those whose sole contact with the organization is through *Along The Line,* which also changed its title a few years back.

Why the changes? Evolution! We are now a far different organization from back in 1968, when we began under yet another name, the Connecticut Valley Railroad Association. Back then, we organized mainly as a spinoff of steam and excursion personnel from the Connecticut Electric Railway Association and the closely allied Connecticut Valley Chapter of the National Railway Historical Society. Our function was to operate railfan excursion runs over various lines of the New Haven Railroad, as the CERA and CVC-NRHS had done during the prior two years, although a number of members had begun to pursue a dream of operating a steam-powered tourist railroad in Connecticut. The CVRA became part of this procedure, a separate organization that would assist in the formation of a new operation. But several obstacles remained for the CVRA at the time: no equipment (engine 97 was privately owned but all equipment was leased from the New Haven), no property (we ran over the New Haven) and most importantly, no adequate funding (steam excursions were not big moneymakers). But there was hope in the form of an alliance with the Empire State Railway Museum of New York, which had not only equipment but a few financially well-off members who generously made the necessary funding available to begin the Valley Railroad project. The years 1969-1971 set this in motion, the CVRA providing much of the volunteer physical effort.

With the VRR Operation off to a successful start, some CVRA members begin to ponder their organization's future goals. The CVRA's role in VRR matters slowly lost importance as the VRR expanded the scope of operation and added paid staff. The CVRA began to concentrate thoughts for its future on the historical end of railroading, slowly expanding a roster of "native" New England equipment. The organization reflected this with its first name change which was phased in beginning in January 1974: the Connecticut Valley Railroad Museum. The CVRM name was adopted as it better stated the purpose of the organization -- the historical preservation of local railroading. Over the following decade, the organization steadily expanded its collection of equipment, artifacts and paperwork. A baggage car was converted into a display car, offering the public a view of what we were all about.

Big changes took place in 1984, with changes in management of both the CVRM and VRR. Much refurbishing of equipment took place, and more creative fundraising by the CVRM enabled a number of historic locomotives to be added to its roster. A formal agreement was signed between the CVRM and VRR, guaranteeing for the first time our presence on the VRR property. Equipment purchases and restorations as well as a series of Railfan Days brought the CVRM national recognition. A location in Old Saybrook was developed by the CVRM for its own use as space at Essex was becoming severely cramped. But by the latter half of the decade, some basic problems resurfaced: Where would we create a "real" railroad museum and how would we support it? And how about our own identity?

By late in 1987, it was decided to adopt a new trade name: The Railroad Museum of New England. While our official organizational name continues as the CVRM, the new RMNE name continues to state our function but also more clearly states the geographic scope of our interests and collection. The following year a study commenced to determine an acceptable location for our future. A number of locations were examined across Connecticut, with final choices being narrowed to remaining at the VRR, Danbury and Willimantic. In the end, it was the people of Willimantic that offered the warmest welcome, and so the decision was made. In 1989, we made our first public appearances in that town, far removed from the Connecticut Valley. So now the time has come once again for the evolution of our name to better state our future. The CVRM name has earned its place in the history or railroad preservation, and now it is time to go forward under the banner of the Railroad Museum of New England.